Doon on a

Doon on a Sunday

David Keeling

Rupa & Co

Copyright © David Keeling 2005

Published 2005 by

Rupa & Co

7/16, Ansari Road, Daryaganj,
New Delhi 110 002

Sales Centres:

Allahabad Bangalore Chandigarh Chennai
Hyderabad Jaipur Kathmandu
Kolkata Mumbai Pune

Typeset in Nikita Overseas Pvt. Ltd.
1410 Chiranjiv Tower
43 Nehru Place
New Delhi 110 019

Printed in India by
Saurabh Printers Pvt. Ltd.
A-16, Sector IV
Noida 201 301

Contents

Acknowledgements

With thanks to M.J. Akbar who told me that I should write. Now it is for the reader to decide whether he was right.

Thanks to Joyeeta Basu of *Asian Age* for editing and titling my articles and to the girls Friday Nilakshi, Sunday Kalyani and Monday Slim Sim for all their suggestions.

Girl Friday went on for her higher studies to St Stephens in Delhi. Sunday, who is now married to a German American, is living in London and Slim Sim who helped finish the book with constant helpful criticism still awaits her fate in Dehra. And to Girl Thursday who is critically reading the manuscript.

Acknowledgements

With thanks to...

Introduction

For those who visit India to see the Taj Mahal, and explore Jaipur, lie on the beaches of Goa and visit New Delhi, they miss out on the mystic world of the Himalayas. And the valley of Doon. This book is about the Himalayas and their resident gods, the valley and its people. Some delightfully idiosyncratic, others bloody temperamental, but all in their own way like Doon Valley, kind and courteous. All presided over by the magnificent and snow-clad peaks of the Himalayas peeking occasionally from the terrace of my cottage.

So, why Dehra Doon? It is a valley, nestling in the lower foothills of the Himalayas at an altitude between two thousand and seven thousand feet. It is now the capital of the newly created state of Uttaranchal. Warm in the summer, it rains ceaselessly in the monsoons and is freezing in the winter. The people, mainly Garhwalis, are kind and hospitable. Although

Dehra gets crowded with an influx of foreigners and locals from the plains and elsewhere, nothing can detract from the wooded hills and the peace and calm of the mountains. In Dehra, everyone has at least one dog which is why it has an abundance of vets. It also has a super-abundance of good schools. It is for this reason that people flock to the 'Queen of the Hills', Mussoorie and Dehra.

An additional dedication and thank you to the Gods of the Himalayas who look over us with amusement but look after us with some benevolence.

1

The Courteous Battle of Kalanga

In the Himalayas, above Rishikesh stands a fairytale castle. Erected in 1910 by the then Maharaja of Tehri, its purpose was solely for entertaining, ostentatiously, the oligarchy of India. With a viceroy thrown in for pudding. It has now been converted and enhanced, inventively, by the hospitable Ashok Khanna as a health spa, The Ananda Himalaya. It is situated in two hundred acres of forest, with views of Doon to make one dream and drool. The food, as expected in a health spa, is both delicious and nutritious. Dehra Doon's inimitable Mona Schwartz provides rice and advice, the macrobiotic way. A delight I have yet to experience. The variety of treatments offered by the spa left me bewildered. 'A marine intensive body blitz trio' followed by a 'hydro foot bath' ending with a 'lap pool'. My body boggled. Electric powered, environmentally sensitive golf carts glide gently through the gardens. Then to the restaurants for refreshment and on to the rooms for repose. Ananda was chock full of guests, mainly consisting, at this time of the year, foreigners including Frederick Forsyth and his family. It is a positive and living demonstration of Uttaranchal's tourist potential. Visitors may come to our state to bathe themselves in the Ganga, for the *aartis* of Rishikesh and Haridwar; or for the sad solemn immersion of ashes. Uttaranchal has more than mad Mussoorie and lazy Landour. So forget Hong Kong and Singapore. Come to see us; and explore.

Doon contains the site of Kalanga. Wooded hills, where the British fought the Gurkhas in 1815. It was a bloody war during which the British were repulsed many times, with ferocity. But the conflict was conducted with amazing decorum. Hari Lal records that a Gurkha soldier, wounded, asked for treatment from British medical staff. He received it with all courtesy. He returned to the Gurkha lines to fight again against the British. The Kalanga fort was pulverised by British artillery. Kalanga is now only a memorial to the dead. The once famous fort is forgotten. The Gurkhas have gone. So too have the British. It was predictable that Friday and I failed to find the fort. Instead, we picnicked by the now winter dry riverbed of the Song. Access to our picnic spot, with a view of the elusive Kalanga hill was via a pedestrian suspension bridge. Friday, keen to demonstrate the principle of this architectural marvel made it sway, alarmingly, by jumping up and down in the middle. On the far bank I was comfortable with chilled Chardonnay. It was a day of unusual silence disturbed only by large trucks heavily laden with rocks from the riverbed. We built a small bush fire surrounded by stones against the chill. And extinguished it safely before leaving. In the dusk, passing through the village of Ladpur we espied a *haveli*. It was too beautiful to pass. The occupant, whose ancestors had been local landowners, was hospitable. The *haveli* is some four hundred years old. Murals on the walls, depicted Lord Vishnu, Ganesha, Krishna frolicking with the *gopis* and panels of peacocks and cobras. The wooden doors and windows had been carved exquisitely, contrasting oddly with a carelessly propped child's bicycle and cricket bat. The *haveli* was strangely silent. Perhaps it was running on its days of glory and glitter.

On a bright, sunlit day in Doon, we made another visit to Mussoorie and Landour. This time using the lesser-trafficked old road. Prettier but precarious in places. First to revisit the Savoy Hotel for tea for Friday and beer for me. A view of the mountains. 'The Banderpunch'. It had already received a fresh overcoat of snow and glistened brilliantly in the sunlight. My old bearer friend was attentive and hoped we might stay the night. Sadly, only one of the few attractions of the Savoy remain.

Their antique furniture and relics which still sparkle. Their damp beds and dubious cuisine do not. On to Landour where Ruskin Bond and his family were their usual selves. Ruskin having recently submitted to a haircut had caught a chill. And so, he did not accompany us to poke around Landour cemetery. Friday still finds it eerie. The ghosts of the long dead and forgotten patiently await new companions. I could be planted there in perfect peace. With these macabre thoughts in mind we departed, me with reluctance, Friday with relief, for a picnic lunch on a grassy knoll under pines, deodars and mountain oak trees. We watched the occasional travellers pass. People looked down, or from side to side, but rarely up, preserving our privacy.

En route to Dehra Doon the silver shops of Landour Bazaar beckoned. There is the occasional treasure still. I found a silver two anna coin dated 1919. How many hands had clasped it, cherished it before its useful life ended. Friday found a coin on which was stamped 'for amusement only.' On the reverse was the head of George V and the legend 'no cash value'.

A rather rude Sardarji, this not being a dichotomy, verbally accosted my wife about the *Dehra Doon Diary*. In particular about my use of the word 'bugger'. I commented that if he had read what I had written with attention he would have comprehended that I was writing about my onions. Every Britisher knows his onions. Under some obscure United

Nations Security Council Resolution, doubtless duplicated by an European Commission Directive, my onions have the same hermaphroditic rights as everyone else. For interested readers may care to know that the Oxford English Dictionary describes 'buggers' as 'Bulgaris, Bulgarians (members of the Greek Church).' So, Sardarji, beware of Greeks bearing fruits, especially from Bulgaria. No point. He wouldn't get it.

2

Dancing in the Dark to Peru's National Anthem

Dehra Doon is replete with societies dedicated to the advancement and enhancement of the valley—'Friends of Doon,' 'Clean Doon' and others. Uttaranchal civil servants try their best to help and humour them. Their political masters are less accommodating. But Looney Doonies don't give up. Whether it is the disposal of waste, lax traffic control or illegal roadside hoardings (now forbidden by the Election Commission), they don't give up. They are intrepid. The hoardings area menace, obscuring views of the valley and of the road. The gods would not approve. One of our principal tireless workers for the removal of these monstrosities, so far with only partial success, is Bunty Chopra. His long and frequently emotional speeches sadly have little effect on the advertising mafia. But he deserves a poem. As does the state government. Ogden Nash in 1933, *Song of the Open Road*:

> I think that I shall never see,
> A billboard lovely as a tree.
> Perhaps, unless the billboards fall,
> I'll never see a tree at all.

Jeeves has pointedly told me that my skin is getting wrinkled in the Himalayan sun. A doctor whom I shall not name under threat of litigation (his solicitors taken from *Private Eye's* Sue, Grabbit & Runne) morosely diagnosed skin cancer. Jeeves reckons old age. So I quote a famous poet anon:

> You're not old
> When your hair grows grey
> You're not old
> When your teeth fall away
> But you're old and it's time
> For a good night's sleep
> When your mind makes
> Suggestions that your body can't keep.......

Driving in Delhi, from Chanakyapuri to my favourite watering hole, the old bar in the IIC, I passed many monuments which Lutyens wouldn't recognise anymore. The environs of the jewel of the Raj have been transformed by an imaginative Punjabi to highlight the India Shining feeling. It looks pretty tardy to me. But, however many times the Delhi administration changes street names, which is increasingly frequent, the roads of Lutyen's Delhi still maintain their precision, symmetry and greenery.

Paris has the Champs Elysee, London its Oxford Street, but they pale in comparison to New Delhi and the view of the Rashtrapati Bhavan on a misty morning from India Gate. Then past Safdarjung's Tomb, imaginatively restored by the Archaeological Survey of India and Intach. Then down past Lodi Gardens, the palms looking scrubbed, barely concealing the magnificent mausoleums and hiding young lovers from the joggers and their dogs. Then to lunch at the IIC with Moni Chadha. He was India's ambassador to Argentina. I ran the Argentine desk in London, but was never allowed a visa by the *junta* because of my past associations with the Falkland Islands. So over lunch, we swapped stories about South America. He had been invited to a wine and beauty festival in a remote area of Tierra del Fuego near the Chilean border. As guest of honour, he was obliged to kiss all the lady contestants. Another onerous diplomatic duty. I reprised with the true tale of one of our first female ambassadors to Uruguay. Who, in her speech, in a fit of effusions decried that she was so happy to be in

Paraguay! And Eartha Kitt, visiting Brazil for the Rio carnival said: 'Gee, shucks, I don't speak Spanish.' Neither did the Brazilians. So we ended with a story, possibly apocryphal, about a former British foreign minister, Lord George Brown who was famous for his tippling and dancing. He would never fly to America, preferring to go by Queen Elizabeth II, as British Airways would not let him dance even in first class. When George went on an official visit to Peru, so Moni was told by a British ambassador, he arrived at his own reception rather late. With four sheets to the wind he espied, through a drunken haze, an elegantly clad person across the room in a long silk ruby robe and immediately lurched across the floor and asked for a dance 'No,' was the response. 'For three reasons. First you are drunk. Second, this is not a waltz, it is the national anthem of Peru and third, I am the Cardinal Archbishop of Lima.'

A warm, if unexpected email from an old, but young Ghanaian friend, Comfort. We used to attend seminars together. She with a human rights group whose name escapes me, I for the Foreign Office. We would listen to learned speakers vividly or vivisectionally describe violations of human rights in Africa. There was always the temptation to yawn, and say 'been there, seen it, done that.' Elderly matrons in their Oxfam sharp cast-offs would demand a statement from the representative of Her Majesty's government. Diplomacy is the art of how to put the unpalatable truth in the most sympathetic way. Yes, I had met Jonas Savimbi, the Angolan rebel leader, and listened to him with disbelief. He was an impressive self-opinionated fanatic, but was he worse than the ruling military government? Also the guerrillas from Mozambique where my minister, the lovely Lynda Chalker brokered a peace, although she kept berating both sides in lousy Spanish. 'They speak Portuguese,' I told her. She replied 'It's all the same. You just need to raise your voice, kiss them on the cheek and smile.' Well, it worked. The Africans went away in awe of her wrath but loved her attention.

So back to Comfort. After a tedious seminar, she would hopscotch through the waiting invitations to eat powdered yam and beans at the Africa Centre and join me for lunch at Gordon's wine bar situated unobtrusively under a toilet of a house where Rudyard Kipling once lived, near Charing Cross Station. Gordon's is still an institution known to few, but always packed by many. Established in 1940, known accurately as the 'The Gay Gordon's,' it sells among other wines, white Portuguese port. The furniture and fittings have hardly changed. Three-legged chairs, two-legged tables, candle-lit and featuring suspicious inedible substances dripping down the walls. The maître d' is Joan who leaves her shopping bags on tables reserved for established clients. Comfort would arrive, to drink wine, white port and talk of cabbages and kings. She is now with UNHCR in Geneva (boring), but better than her previous assignment with UNIFEM in New York. I urge her to come to Delhi to supplement the vast UN complex in Max Mueller Bhavan next to the India International Centre. A breath of fresh air from Comfort even in the back of a mandatory Merc would do the UN some good.

3

Mussoorie: An Affair to Remember

This is about Mussoorie and its people. I quote from Ruskin's book on Mussoorie. 'Mussoorie has a great tradition of romance. It was where you went to do your own thing, indulge in a secret love affair, or build a cottage for your mistress. Sometimes the superior officer turned up, hoping to get away from the eyes of his junior officers. And if ever the twain met, well they looked the other way.' Sadly no longer. Pushy 'Yaars' take away your peace. A secret love affair? With overfed, overeager, overbearing wives watching? You must be joking. Build a cottage at present day land prices? Forget it. Sorry Ruskin. We were born too late.

The National Society for Promotion of Development Administration, Research & Training, a wing of the Lal

Bahadur Shastri Academy of Administration is located in Landour in the quaintly named Cozy Nook. Girl Friday and I were invited to visit the Academy by the Director, Dr Atindra Sen. I met him as usual, with other interesting passengers on the Mussoorie Express, where one meets all the nicest new people in one's life. Finally, I had expected to attend a conference of chief secretaries to discuss the Government of India's new education policy. This, we found had been abruptly cancelled. But we were made very welcome at the academy. Naturally, apart from me the only three other people present, the Andhra Pradesh Chief Secretary (education), the Director and Girl Friday, were all old Stephanians. They instinctively recognised each other. Swapped names, college experiences and traded tales of their respective Stephanian experiences not withstanding the age gaps. Englishmen recognise each other by their school ties. Stephanians needed no such sophistry.

> *If you go down to the woods today, you're in for a big*
> *   surprise.*
> *If you go down to the woods today, you'd better go in*
> *   disguise.*
> *For today was the day of the Woodies Annual Picnic.*

So might have run the teddy bears' nursery rhyme, and is an apt introduction to the Woodstock school's reunion dinner for the Class of 1951, hosted by the hospitable Bob and Ellen Alter at their house in Landour. Bob is a former headmaster of Woodstock. Girl Friday and I attended. We were made most welcome. I in a suit and tie, for the first time in months. Girl Friday with her arm in a sling. Writer's cramp or possibly a bid to gain sympathy from the Woodies. She succeeded.

It was a glorious evening. I sat and listened to the endless, fascinating reminiscences from old Woodies who had gathered from all over the world. Many of the spouses were visiting India for the first time. It showed. Stars in their eyes. By the end one was moved to murmur, 'For ever with thou love, and she be fair.' So they had one for the road and will come back for more.

Antique shops from those of Portobello Road to Print Market in Hong-Kong and finally to Landour Bazaar have dubious ware. Real or manufactured in Moradabad? But does the Delhite really care? Stick it on your wall even if it says on the back 'Made in Mussoorie'. Kolkata and Mumbai flea markets have some treasures to be found. But they are for the discerning, not the dealers. In London at Christie's I stopped bidding for antiques at their auction of Indian British memorabilia because an avaricious Indian from New Delhi, South Extension, continuously and deliberately outbid me. He would, of course sell his finds at a vastly inflated profit to ignorant nouveau riche Delhi residents with more money than sense.

I got wise to this wheeler dealer. Lunched with a lovely Christie's Caroline. Told her of my problem. She told me that there was a big box of rubbish in the next sale of British Indian artefacts. The New Delhi, South Extension man would not be interested in old pots and pans. But beneath this old pile of colonial rubbish I found two sets of beautiful solid silver knives and forks. The Christie's lady bid on my behalf. I won. Dehra Doon 1, New Delhi, South Extension 0.

Doon was once owned by emperors and princes. At one time part of Aurangzeb's empire, he gifted the Doon Valley to Guru Ram Rai. Aurangzeb's description of the Doon and Mussoorie, written in 1708, is graphic and beautiful. It still has its Maharaja's mansions although most are now rarely used. Mayfair now, not Mussoorie, for the monied. Back to Guru Ram Rai. I have previously quoted an excerpt translated into English from Aurangzeb's inscription in Persian on the Guru's memorial *gurudwara* in Dehra Doon. I make no apology for quoting another with reference to Landour and Mussoorie as they should be seen;

Bound on one side by mountains,
and the other by thick forests...
On each side of this place springs and bubbles
With stream of flowing water
..... to see Paradise on earth, see this

But please, welcome visitors, before you leave us, spare a few moments to collect your litter. Leaving us as lovely as you found us.

Next morning, Girl Friday and I went to meet Ruskin Bond in his cottage which is perched above a potential 'lovers leap'. Hold hands, jump and you can forget about the dowry. Ruskin took us on a conducted tour of the old Landour Cemetery, still occasionally in use but now more often macabrely used as a picnic spot. The Landour Cemetery is a place of secret silence, a tribute to men and women and their children who died and were buried there nearly two hundred years ago. Tall green deodars stand as silent sentinels over the moss laden tombstones. In one corner stands a plaque with the inscription, 'planted by the Duke of Edinburgh in 1870'. Further ahead lies the mortal remains of Elizabeth Heely. She died, eighteen months old. In 1840 bereaved parents were moved to inscribe on their daughter's grave, 'The Lord giveth and the Lord taketh. Blessed be the name of the Lord'. I doubt whether I would be so tolerant of the Lord, having lost my only child.

Ruskin told us that the earliest grave dated from 1820. On that day, with a wire brush and eerie instinct we discovered a plaque in an old mossy wall dated 1810. Ruskin was perplexed but excited. Dehra Doon and Landour did not exist as British Cantonments in 1810. Another mystery to be unravelled. We speculated. Ruskin hazarded that the deceased was a hapless visitor from Saharanpur, the then headquarters of the British Botanical Society who had had an accident. Girl Friday, with relish, speculated that he might have been eaten by a tiger. The hunter being consumed by the hunted!

Old, young, rich and poor. Beautiful and plain. Soldiers and sweethearts. Husbands and wives. Some who did indeed 'drink life to the lees'. Others who had been barely granted a glimpse. They all rest here together, forgotten not forsaken, in eternity. Waiting for the trumpets of Judgement Day. Quietly, the wind blows, startling a woodpecker into flight, to the relief of the cypress tree. Saying farewell to Ruskin, Girl Friday was standing on the lintel of the cemetery gate. A flutter by espying a lonely, kindred spirit dropped by. A farewell flourish of amber and rust.

4

Sisterly Tales:
How to Raise Hair at Landour

It was time to vary my routine. It was too wet for golf so with alacrity I accepted an invitation to lunch with Parul Prakash in Sisters Bazaar, Landour. Parul's shop is situated next door to the famous Prakash store, with its cheese and jams. Parul has a handicraft shop with books on sale. Both are worth a visit. Parul's place is stocked with items made by the less privileged for the financially more privileged. Sisters Bazaar is named after the nursing sisters who lived there while servicing the then British Military Hospital in Landour. It is a long treacherous drive, well above the vulgarity of Mussoorie. Dev Anand has a house there, though he rarely visits. So does Prannoy Roy. Sisters Bazaar has only two shops. Both owned by the Prakash family. Not too surprising. Last winter they had no *bijli, pani,* or telephone for two weeks. And were snowbound. Parul took me for a preprandial walk. Then a good veg lunch with the delightful Mrs Prakash, Parul's mother, I took them some of my ominous jackfruits beginning to intrude like Wyndham's Triffids. Then a hair raising drive down the mountains from seven thousand five hundred feet to three thousand in an hour.

A story in *The Asian Age* was about the intrepid scooter ladies in Dehra Doon. The ones who carve up to me and the other obnoxious drivers with skill and daring. I asked the two for an interview. They were not what I expected. Vidushi Arora is in her second year at LSR, Commerce and Arts. A delightful young lady, a Doonite with her mind firmly fixed on her career. Not for the *HT* wedding column. But Vidushi does not drive the scooter. Her friend and mentor, Mrs Angela Beattie a Canadian BA and MA on an American research project, drives. Vidushi shouts insults at intrusive road hogs.

Angela is in Dehra Doon doing research for her PhD on the subject of 'infant massage.' Complete news to me, but now very much in fashion in the US. Vidushi helps in translations. I had only heard about immersing babies in swimming pools shortly after birth. In America they have learnt of 'infant massage' supposedly very common in India. *Ayahs*, mothers and grandparents. My daughter, calling from Australia tells me that it is a common practice there too. Massage the baby, having learnt the basics, and the child will benefit. Sounds like a good idea, but consult your doctor. In Doon Dr Pandhi will advise.

After a sad and deeply regrettable episode in Oldham, how good it was to watch the friendly behaviour of Pakistan, Indian and British supporters of cricket at Old Trafford. No football type segregation. Does cricket civilise? And does cricket diplomacy work?

So another Sunday in the Doon ebbs and flows. Delightfully cool. Music. Writing. Reading. Friends drop in uninvited. Life is good in Doon.

5

Trust Me, I Was Not Man-Handled

I am, courtesy of Mike Dalvi, becoming another Doon resident to acquire a dog. A lovely Labrador. Most dogs like me, and I reciprocate, except for a yappy, yuppy, nippy little mongrel owned by my sister-in-law in Delhi. It and I do not get along. And two nascent Rottweiler puppies, recently bought by a next-door neighbour, which being outside provide better and more vocal protection than a sleeping watchman. Rather like the Greeks of ancient days who used geese as an early warning system against invaders. Sati and Renu Puri, most hospitable neighbours have a dog who basked comfortably in my *godi*. The dog occasionally pretended to lick my ear while surreptitiously sniffing my beer. I forget the dog's name, but names can be quite misleading. Once, in London, we held a dinner party for the Rasgotras, the then Indian high commissioner. Mrs Rasgotra's pet name was Chhoti. So was that of our diminutive Nepalese maid. The latter a great favourite with our guests. 'Chhoti,' cries would ring through the garden. '*Ek aur drink lao!*' Mrs Rasgotra was not amused. I quickly and quietly replenished Krishna Rasgotra's drink, before he joined the chorus. He looked faintly disappointed. I shall call my doggie 'Fred.'

Now the New Year's story. In Auli, where there are few trucks and buses especially during the winter, the villagers told me of the hardship they endure. But they had learnt from a local newspaper of a new economic programme being introduced by the Uttaranchal state government. This reminds me of one of the famous Hungarian stories. The then communist Hungarian government was irritated by the Czechoslovakian attempt (under Alexander Dubeck) of gaining freedom from the Russians (they thought that they should have done it first). They introduced a new economic mechanism. As usual, in Hungary, every government initiative was greeted in cafes and taverns at lunchtime with a joke. This one is appropriate for the *patwari*. The villages, not understanding the new economic system, asked the *patwari* to explain how it would benefit them. The *patwari* was nonplussed. He hadn't a clue, but his clever wife came to the rescue. We will go to Dehra Doon for discussions, she announced. And some shopping she thought. The *patwari* was received courteously and after an hour the minister arrived. 'Sitting here,' he asked, how many lorries full of grain have passed while you were waiting?' 'Two,' replied the *patwari*. Said the minister, 'After the economic reforms there will be twenty.' The *patwari* returned to Auli no wiser. There were no trucks of grain in his village either in summer or in winter. He sat gloomily waiting for words of wisdom. Two beggars passed. Inspiration. The villagers assembled and waited. The *patwari* asked, 'How many beggars have passed in the last hour?' 'Two,' was the reply. The rest you can guess.

Once or twice a year, Girl Sunday gives a dinner dance for the clan of the Badola's. It is extensive, the late and lamented Mr Badola having squired ten children. A bit like my goldfish. They, like the goldfish are equally productive. So when Kalyani had her December dinner dance, the company was Badola's and Badola's and Badola's, world wide. Did I as the only foreigner and not a Badola feel out of place? Not a bit. We all had something in common. In fact lots of things. We were freezing cold. Several of her male cousins and her brothers asked me to dance. In the most friendly way. I have never before danced with a man, although there was no hugging and kissing. Thank god! It was the latest evening party and one of the most enjoyable that I had attended in Dehra Doon. The food kept coming. The main course at midnight. Angeethi carefully placed radiating heat. After the main course, it was time for momentous Black Forest cake which was delicious if hardly something to diminish the waistline. Another evening of delight in Doon though not for the cab driver.

Girl Sunday decided that she needed a chest of drawers for her bedroom. Naturally antique, no Saharanpur modern rubbish she says. A piece of furniture with lots of drawers and a mirror in which she could admire herself. 'Mirror mirror on the wall, who is the fairest of them all?' The mirror remained sullenly silent. Nor did I fare better. So we repaired up the familiar road to Mussoorie to an antique shop owned by Irfan Ahmed. There Sunday, found what she was looking for, tucked away in the corner. I asked the proprietor whether this was a genuine antique and he assured me that it was. On a previous trip to one of the many antique shops there, we had watched workers laboriously drilling fake worm holes in the woodwork and applying coats of varnish before beating and authenticating aging process with chains.

Poking around the dusty shop, my eye caught a curious wooden box. The proprietor opened it to reveal its secrets. It must have originally been a travelling writing chest for some British or ICS officer. The woodwork, brass bound, was beautifully maintained. There were drawers, compartments and more drawers. All crafted in antique mahogany. We noticed, having taken out most of the drawers, there was something missing. An empty space in the base. With some dexterity and ingenuity we found an unobtrusive device which unlocked the rest of the magic box. Other drawers slid in and out. Sunday found three more. There is one remaining, the entry to which is still a mystery yet to be solved. My secret box. Every school child's dream. I shall collect boxes and become a true boxwallah.

Nayantara Sehgal, who needs no introduction, is together with her sister-in-law and Mangat Rai some of my many illustrious neighbours on Rajpur Road. Mangat Rai passed away recently at a respectable age of eighty-seven. He was a renowned member of the ICS both in Bihar and Punjab where he worked with Dharam Viraji, the then governor. Another of my neighbours, Jagdish Prasad, uncertain on his feet after a long illness, clinging firmly to my hand, and I called to offer condolences. After a farewell to the body, we sat in the sun for half an hour. Mangat Rai was a Church of England Christian. He had wanted to be buried in his garden. Too difficult, decreed the authorities. So Nayantara Sehgal told us that Rai had asked for his remains to be disposed of with the least hassel to anyone and with a prayer by a priest from St Joseph's church. It is, said Mrs Sehgal, the memories of life that count. Mangat Rai, courteous in life, was thoughtful in death, R.I.P.

6

Teddy Bears' Picnic at Bitter Waters

The winds of March have changed into glorious sunshine. Hot, with the fish eager to procreate. The papaya is now ready and ripe for their covering of newspaper to be stripped and the fruit ready for breakfast with *nimbu* dressing. Freddie is still mad at the monkeys. A return match is imminent, just as exciting as the Indian Pakistan cricket tour. Winter woollens away. Back to summer shorts. Cumulus climb the *chota* Himalayas soon to dissipate in the heat and never to return. Birds in abundance chirping merrily. Petunias and frangipani displace the depleting crocus. The lychee tree promises a bumper crop. To be peeled and gutted by Miss Maali sitting cross-legged before she takes them for canning. So the sprightly step returns. Love comes later.

Sunday in Doon on 29th February, a leap year, so Freddie leaped, but only proposed a union with my cashmere sweater. My newly band-boxed Pringle was soon a mass of golden Lab hair. There is something especial about Pringle Kashmiri sweaters from Scotland although, I am told that they are now manufactured in Ludhiana. Certainly our Pringle shop in Dehra Doon doesn't seem to quite meet the criteria. 'Every time I wear my Pringle, it gives me a little extra tingle'.

The ice-box loaded, Jeeves, Qualis and I went to meet the Loony Doonies for their annual picnic. The meeting was at the Doon Club into which Jeeves drove stylishly by the gate from which one is supposed to exit. An irate *chowkidar* was appalled. Clad like a sugar plum fairy in white *churidars* and an orange *pagdee*, he was definitely Bollywood material. 'Go back' he said. 'Piss off,' I replied genially. He did. The Loony Doonies picnic is never bereft of trauma. We left for the picnic which was a short drive through the forest to a rest house surrounded by sal wood. Naturally on the forest road, an enterprising contractor had overturned a large container full of God knows what into the ditch thereby blocking all the traffic. Two large cranes arrived (the motorised version not the birds), but were unable to help. Impetuous traffic and buses built up. Maruti's tried the short cut only to find mud in the cud. Resigned to my fate, I sang *The Teddy Bear's Picnic* with an appreciative audience of young kids who had invaded the Qualis. While refreshing myself with a restorative gin and tonic, we eventually arrived at the entrance to the forest when of course, the gate was locked. A forest guard was eventually dragged out from the *chai* stall nearby and he reluctantly admitted that we were expected. We all had to fill in forms which described our vehicles, sex and purpose of visit. Then pay a fee. Fifteen kilometres later, we arrived at the rest house of Karwa Pani known as Bitter Waters which as the saying goes, the local *patwari* used it for his ablutions. Here too, the gates were similarly locked. This was obviously a family cartel. The same rigmarole until we established the sanctity of the rest house. Mr Rajan Brijnath gave us instructions. Sensible ones like, children walking in the forest must be accompanies by adults. But then 'Adults go around in pairs'. Childhood memory sent me into a paroxysm of giggles, earning a stern look from the chef de tour. It went, sung to the tune of the Eton College boating song, *'we're all friends together, we go around in pairs. We're all friends together, excuse us while we go upstairs.'* I sung it sotto voce to a sprightly elderly lady sitting next to me. She looked at me strangely and laughed, croaking like a frog. Her husband, as a boy, had been a pupil at Eton. After lunch, Rajan organised the inevitable quiz for the *bacha's* who were completely ignorant of the questions. Florence Pandi proposed a compromise in that, the kids would confront the judges (of whom I was one) performing impromptu sketches entitled,' Tiger eats a man', 'Monkeys in the forests' and,' Wild elephants approach'. I awarded maximum marks to Team C whose vocal rendition of wild elephants was truly frightening. So the Loony Doonies went home through the gathering dusk to find, miraculously all the forest gates open, the roadside accident removed. An end to another perfect day.

It was with some trepidation that in Delhi, I listened to advice from lawyers, friends and succinctly newly acquired family members to make my will. Naturally, stacked in their favour. Making a will seems so final although my plot on Camel's Back in Mussoorie is already booked. With an alternative at St John's Church in the Wilderness near Mcleod Gunj in Himachal. The last offers stupendous views although the coffin has to be raised for them to be truly appreciated. A Lord Elgin is buried there after having lost the family marbles while unwisely crossing a river ropeway. But back to the will. I did the draft in thirty seconds. No way! We had to have it Indian style, 'In sound disposing state of mind' and naturally codicil's. And to declare, this is my last will and device. And a bonus on signing, I became a testator prior to the end. Witnessed by a lawyer and a doctor. Just in case I should change my mind.

Mao Shergill telephoned the cottage inviting me to the ceremony of his inauguration as new Chairman of Punjab Public Service Commission in Chandigarh. Could I refuse,

I asked Girl Sunday. 'No,' she said, 'and anyways, I will be busy'. Ashok Massey dropped in to share pizza and a garden salad. I asked him about the road to Chandigarh which he assured me was fine. Wrong! It was a pretty road but with surfaces so uneven that the sturdy Qualis shuddered. Eventually arrived in Chandigarh, and I was never a fan of Corbusier. No street maps, only Orwellian sectors, never in sequence. I arrived at the Governor's residence, somewhat late having stopped to be suited and tied at the Sunbeam Hotel. I was given a warm welcome. Outside the forbidding guarded gates, an I.P.S. Officer appeared as if by magic. 'Are you Mr David from Dehra Doon?' Doors were opened. Jeeves and Qualis drove past a fleet of red-helmeted Ambassadors to our specially planned parking place. I was, courtesy of Mao Shergill, introduced to a guy who had personally shot five tanks in the 1982 war. He got a P.V.S.M. 'Shouldn't you have got five?' I asked. He couldn't really speak fluent English. But he sure as hell could shoot tanks.

7

New Year Resolutions: Gone with the Hangover

Doon for New Year 2005 excelled and chilled. Parties galore, the first in a friends' garden, in the warming if watery sunshine, looking up at the crystal clear mountains of Mussoorie, from where the snow on the mall had cleared. Much to the disappointment of the *bachchas*. So back from the soggy snowballs of the Himalayas to the more durable cricket balls of Jalandhar. Promptly at three-thirty, lunch barely consumed, the gods brought an end to the festivities with icy rain drops. We retreated to the cottage for a log fire, mince pies, brandy butter and tea. The snow drops and crocus seemed to revel in the cold. Perhaps they are of Garhwali stock from long past. So, I eschewed Nita Roy's New Year's bash for a 'hottie,' a book and bed. With the *Arrival of the Queen of Sheba* on tape. Freddie had long since departed to the land of nod, having given me a salivating slurp. I soon joined him.

We had a party during that no-man's land between Christmas and New Year. Despite the freezing cold, dear Lillian Skinner and her great-grandnephew journeyed to join us from Barlowganj. The Shamsher Singhs, Billimorias, Shergills, the new IMA commandant Lt Gen Negi whose wife got a broken bone while paragliding or some such thing. But it shows the gentlemen cadets what is in store for them and their wives. Four generals reminiscent of Sir Richard Attenborough's *Oh What a Lovely War!* and *Gandhi*. The cream of the Indian Military regaled us with stories. How Billy Billimoria, escorting the Dalai Lama and the Panchen Lama in India in the 1950s had kindly explained to the young Panchen the use of a miniature *kukri*. Holding it in his hand, Billy was promptly arrested for attempting to do away with the young boy. Needless to say, he was exonerated with profuse apologies from the Dalai Lama. Sujeet Das, home secretary, and his delightful wife answered questions with their usual polish and diplomatic aplomb which must be taught, as it was to us in England, at its equivalent. The Lal Bahadur Shastri Institute on Cosy Nook in Mussoorie. Jeet Banerjee and his wife, the former endlessly retelling his advice to a junior Air Force officer, how, in his retirement he could become an Air Marshal. 'All aeroplanes now have them,' he said.

The Uttaranchal state PWD, probably anticipating heavy traffic and having closed Suicide Alley on Chakrata Road, thought that they would have fun. So they dug up the main Rishikesh road and lined it with bulldozers, steamrollers and those large machines which emit tar macadam. And to add spice, simultaneously on both sides of the road. Various employees lounge around with green and red flags. Obviously colour blind, waving both with uncertainty. The steamroller drivers stopped abreast of each other while the drivers exchanged reminiscences. Two bullock carts, laden with lethal iron rods were shepherded into the traffic. One PWD employee smoking a *bidi* dangerously near the tar container and diesel eventually waved us along with a red flag. We gladly complied. Later, a surely illegal barrier demanded Rs 10 for passage. I had, with Girl Friday, encountered this before. 'Military,' she had snarled. The barrier was opened. Friday sat back, looking satisfied. This time I shouted, 'Official.' No payment. Well, official in a way I was. On the return from Anandas, as an astute guy intercepted the man demanding the loot. 'Official,' he said. The barrier opened. Poor tourists. But they can afford it. I can't.

Ananda Spa is still the most beautiful retreat I have seen in North India. But this was a family lunch, with kids running wild which was both delightful and delicious. Western food, good pomfret from Mumbai, plum pudding and conversation. The Khannas are shortly opening a spa in Mauritius and another in Dubai. There is also a resort in Bangalore. It is a world market and one in which I hope Uttaranchal cashes in.

Now away from parties to New Year's resolutions. A quote from Thomas Russel Ybrra, which applies by no means only to Christians:

> *A Christian is a man who feels*
> *Repentance on a Sunday*
> *For what he did on Saturday night*
> *And will do again on Monday.*

Most of our solemn resolutions wither and die on the vine before the Christmas decorations are dismantled. My resolutions do. Give up booze, smoking; be nice to mother-in-law, stop spending the family fortunes on *taash* at the club. Most are forgotten after the New Year hangover. 'All the world is mad,' said my late father, 'except for us two. Well, I am not and nor are you. But sometimes I wonder about you.

8

But Antique Suits Me, It Also Boots Me

My brother-in-law and his partner while passing through on their way to Mussoorie had dropped in to see and appreciate my cottage in Doon. They gave me a book by Kiran Desai titled *Hullabaloo*. I shan't try to review it. Rushdie has already done so in pompous prose. Welcome proof that India's encounter with the English language has given birth to new children. 'Tosh,' as Bertie Wooster would have said to Jeeves. But Ms Desai's book is a good read. Described in the *New Yorker* as 'a lavish, sharp-eyed fabulist whose send up of small time culture cuts to the heart of human perversity,' 'Praise the Lord,' says Sunday, 'I don't want to be one of those.' Critics retire hurt.

I went to Delhi for two book launches, one by William Dalymple on his latest epic describing how an English officer, in the nineteenth century fell in love with a begum from Hyderabad. He might well have written about the French Lieutenant who married a begum in Meerut. When he died, she built as a memorial, a cathedral in catholic style, but with minarets and staffed by Italian priests. And retired regretfully into purdah. It is still maintained as a magnificent memorial to her love.

To add to William's stories about inter-racial marriages, there was an English Gentlemen, John Baynon who owned hotels in Kulu valley. One morning he espied a young tribal girl brushing the lawn of leaves, and after several days, fell in love with her; they were married. So it is not with only the pomp and ceremony of Hyderabad that mixed marriages can take place. They do so more in simple pictures. Willie, whom I know well, insisted on giving a lecture on his deep and pro-found knowledge on the subject. I fell shortly somnambulantly asleep. I do not like lectures. Give me a *dana* or a *hartaal* any day. Much more fun.

Catherine Young's book launch was, by comparison much less serious and more fun. Although the lawns of the Maurya Hotel in the evening were bloody freezing, a very pleasant crew of people assembled to wish her venture well. I shall not drop names, but many of the great and good graced the occasion. I left early for Old Delhi railway station having forgotten to take copies of Catherine's book which will be delivered to me in Doon. Meanwhile, in the comfort of Northern railways, I read Robert Ludlum and arrived refreshed to the valley.

It's all go in Doon after the monsoon. I was invited to the IMA Commandant's daughter's wedding. I donned my best Simpson's suit, Coles shirt, gold cuff-links, club tie and brightly polished brogue shoes. Nor was I overdressed, although, I forgot to pluck a rose for my buttonhole. My attire reminded Girl Sunday of a jumble sale that she went to when little. She got it nearly right. Not jumble, but certainly antique. I thankfully remembered to take a small wedding gift. The bride was attractively adorned, the bridegroom awed. The ceremony was dignified. No heaving crowds. No booze. Old military friends, now long retired, remembered the days and chatted while their wives eyed me speculatively.

A Kolkata friend—Doon is full of retired Bengali boxwallahs —telephoned to comment on my diary item about Jyoti Basu's suggested change in dress code. 'Does that,' he asked, 'make Mr Basu into a WOG?' This has become one of the most odious, pejorative and derisive descriptions of a person from South Asia. But, originally, it was not. Wog stands for Westernised Oriental Gentleman. Not that I would refer to my Indian friends and families as wogs. But they are, in the original sense. With emphasis on the 'gentleman.' And to carry on with my acronym trail, take 'posh'. Not as in Spice, Beckham fans. Setting out for India by sea when P&O ran real ships and not just cruise liners, the British would go 'posh'. On the journey out, and especially through the Suez Canal, the sun would beat down on the starboard side of the vessel. So, one would travel in a cabin on the port side. Returning home with the sun in the opposite direction, one would travel in a cabin on the starboard side. Thus, Port Out and Starboard Home. POSH.

> On yonder hill there stands a temple
> Who lives there I do not know
> Will it be a fair young maiden?
> Will she answer yes or no?

This is a class rhyme learned by English school children. Across the cud and the always dry riverbed, there are in the misty hills several curious constructions. One of which is a lofty temple. Who lives there if anyone? I will find out. And maybe, buy it to add to an impressive list of unusual land acquisitions.

Returning to Doon by the Northern Railways, I had three gentlemen from ONGC as companions. They were on their way to the Lal Bahadur Shastri College in Cosy Nook near Mussoorie. They discussed their exploits, discovering new oil and natural gas finds in India. If only I was an industrial spy I could have made a fortune. But instead, I secretly sipped my Old Monk and read my book. At the station, Jeeves proprietorially possessed my briefcase. A coolie, my luggage. The cottage was glowing, wood floors gleaming. The log fire winking. The stars twinkling. Home to Doon.

9

Why Candy is Dandy, But Liquor is Quicker

Delhi again by car. Although the journey for me and my readers is getting pretty boring. Except for NH 58, the main highway is as exciting and hairy as a Hindi movie without Preity Zinta. Not that the latter is, I am told, hairy. But she is very pretty.

In Delhi, it was de rigueur to dine with Karan Thapar. There were lots of lady guests who left me quietly to spend time with Mallika Akbar whose serene South Indian eyes either prompt me into talking indiscretions or bite my tongue just in time. 'Come to Doon,' I said. Mallika is a psychotherapist. There are lots of patients here worthy of her treatment.

The new Pakistani High Commissioner was most impressive. Previously posted in Afghanistan. The Indian and

Pakistani foreign ministries vie to post their most senior and presentable diplomats across the border. Earlier, the Lambas from Delhi and now Khan from Pakistan, all well received in both capitals, at least on the surface. Aziz Khan confided that he was more optimistic about the success of the Indo-Pakistan joint initiative. We both hoped so. And planned to play golf in Gulmarg. But I suspect that there will be more security *wallahs* than Agarwalas. I guess that there will be plenty of 'hot drinks' as the girls in Nigeria used to demand on the 19th hole.

This fortnight's real story was yet another visitor to Doon from the ladbrooke Arms in Notting Hill Gate. Dr John, a plastic surgeon from Australia, but now practicing in England is known as 'John the Cut'. A newcomer to India, he fell into our society like a pig in a pudding. I've never seen anyone eat so much. At Moti Mahal in Delhi, he was groaning for food and on the way to Doon, he voraciously scoffed the prepared sandwiches and then went to replenish again at Cheetal. In Doon for Kalyan's birthday, he took us for dinner and every plate was scraped and cleaned.

The next day for breakfast. Dr John attacked bacon. Good stuff from Nepal. Chips, tomatoes, fruit, toast and coffee. Australians are still wary of eggs. Then, in the garden with Freddie before gin and tonic and a journey to the Glasshouse on the Ganges. The excellent food and service did not deter him from taking a dip in the Mother Ganga below. On the way back, nursing another gin and tonic and a bottle of Ganges water, the long drops into the valley below which had worried him on the outward journey, were forgotten. This, he said, was the way to travel. Jeeves, replete from the local Dhaba grinned. Funny foreigners.

The following evening, there was a dinner for John. A cross section of Doon while I was seriously (well almost) sick. So, John was host while I was covered in *razai's* in bed. Jeeves cooked. I could hear the merriment from my pit. Nayantara Sehgal kindly came and said goodnight and thank you. The next day, John's last in Doon, he went to the leprosy mission and returned late. Once Ashok Massey gets you into his clutches, it is difficult to escape his enthusiasm. Honey and Shamsher Singh had invited us for drinks, but Shamsher had already left for obligatory golf. Honey and her daughter Cherry said notwithstanding, to come for a drink. We did in their lovely estate above Rajpur. What was an intended short stay turned into an hour plus. Pink gins and reminisces. Her grandson treated us with a bucketful of turtles recently arrived from parts unknown, the transport master minded by the gods. 'Turn Turtle' said Honey. And they did.

Toothpick Award for this month goes to the Central government's road and highways department. They are building new roads and giving their efforts a great deal of publicity. A full-page advertisement in recent national newspapers showed a new road programme with vivid photographs. A four-lane highway linking every part of India. On the right side was a photograph of the new development and of a truck overtaking a bus. Further down the highway, a flat top lorry was overtaking another truck. No cars in sight. Well, a scooter. So to corrupt Chesterton (Sorry, G.K.):

> A merry road, a rolling road
> Which up the Moguls travelled
> But as of now, the roads Department
> Have much to get unravelled.

A young man, a sort of cousin in Doon, asked me for advice. There was, as usual, this girl. Should he invite her to a coffee shop for snacks and chatter? Buy her flowers or sweets? I remembered the same dilemma in my youth. A friend advised me to take her to watch a cricket match, 'she will be so bored and sleep in your *godi.*' The young boy looked convinced. 'And chocolates? He asked. So to Ogden Nash, 'Candy is dandy. But liquor is quicker'. He didn't get it, but at eighteen, neither did I.

10

House-Proud: Oakless in Oak Land

'I was a precious child,' said Maharani Prithivi Bir Kaur of Jind. The Raj Mata, as she has now become, lives in an elegant house called, appropriately 'Oakless'. No oak trees. She had just returned from her devotions to the Sai Baba in Puttaparthi. Bill Aitken was in attendance, although he is not, she said sadly, a devotee. We sat chatting over a glass of Himachal apple juice followed by a sample from the Scottish highlands. And we were asked to use her pet name, Raj Ma. Her description of herself as a precious child was quite right. At fifteen she fell in love with her mother's half brother. They eloped and were married in Kashmir. This was the high spot in the lovely lady's life. The Jind Maharaj had two wives, she being the junior. And she, by tradition, was obliged to stand when the senior wife entered the room. Raj Ma was eventually recognised by the British as a Maharani. And subsequently as Raj Mata. She played the piano, western, pop and classical, but stopped when her husband objected. She no longer plays. Raj Ma is a firm devotee of the Sai Baba. Kalyani is too. Sai Baba stayed for two nights at Oakless with the Raj Mata near Barlowgunj; and she has lovely pictures of Baba and even more beautiful memories of his stay there. And the room in which he rested and which she cherishes. We left, clutching a photograph of Sai Baba, and was gifted with a small packet of Baba's *vibhuti*.

A semi-permanent guest at Oakless is Bill Aitken, the famous travel writer. He and Raj Mata have known each other for years and stay companionably in the hills. Bill is an inveterate trekker. His last planned adventure was stymied because his servant got mugged. But he will try again. I think that the approaches to Nanda Devi are to him as challenging as those of the Raj Mata to Sai Baba. Each to his own.

In 1871, the Reverend Brother Jacoby established a monastery whose missionaries from Italy were inspired by St Francis of Assisi. It still exists and is now run by the Reverend Father Hugh Tharakan. Adjacent is a church dedicated to St Michael the Archangel, whose fresco adorns the main altar. The cemetery, and I apologise if I write so much about places of death, has in it planted many who have descended in this earth by virtue of their following the faith. Rest in peace. The monastery is now a place for retreats, recreation and reading. Situated at the centre of the campus of one of North India's schools, it will be quiet and peaceful during the summer, but more boisterous in term time. The Reverend Brother gives learned lessons to those who listen.

The resurgent monastery is now enclosed by St George's College. A predominantly Roman Catholic school, it is one of the finest in North India. Preference is given, the principal told us to children from a Catholic background, although religion is no bar. It was established by Bishop Daniel Delany, born in 1747. From the J.P. Residency Hotel terrace, the college looms impressively. A Gothic frontage with Mughal turrets is surmounted by a huge chiming clock. A Big Ben replica. Which surprisingly stays on time. The principal gave us free reign of the campus which is constructed dramatically overlooking the valley of Doon. With Lal Tibba and Dhanaulti coyly hiding in the clouds above. St George's was funded by missionaries, like many schools in North India, but in this case, by the Irish. St George with his dragon is the patron saint of England. The Irish drink of black gold, dear to English hearts, is sadly not brewed at St George's.

11

Buffalo Tales:
When One and Two Make Half

The Commandant of IMA, Lt Gen Shergill very kindly offered us access to the academy libraries. Browsing, Girl Friday found a photograph of the IMA Angling Club. This was established by Col M.A.R. Skinner in 1953. Then a Major, Skinner caught a fish weighing thirty-five and a half pounds, the first Mahaseer of the season. This was a feat, but to hold it up with one hand, on display for the photographer was an even greater achievement.

The Skinner family still lives in Northern India. Jim Skinner stays in a crumbling residence in Hansi. His sister, Mrs Lillian Skinner Singh lives near Mussoorie. We went to meet her. She had agreed to see us with some trepidation.

William Dalrymple had wrongly and unkindly written of her home as a Baronial Mansion. It is in fact a colonial house, beautifully and comfortably furnished and decorated without any trappings of a Maharaja. As so often happens in India, large families have poor relations. Lillian's grand aunt Alice, whom Lillan described as clever, conscientious but of plain looks (shades of Jane Austen perhaps), was determined that her poor relatives should have somewhere substantial to live, in which they could be secure. So Sikander Hall was constructed. Named after the rallying call of 'Skinner's Horse,' 'Skinner Sahib.' Lillian still lives there. I expected Lillian Skinner Singh to be interesting. I was wrong. She is a gem. And sparkled. Within a few minutes, with good humour and jokes aplenty, she told us her own story. Her great grandfather Alexander Skinner, who died in 1887, bought from an aptly named Mr Rich, properties named Midstream, Oaklane and Airfield. The last now houses the Nabha Hotel. In those days one did not buy a *bigha* but something bigger. A mountain. But more about Lillian's sense of humour. She laughs continuously and explosively. But first, she says, you must know how to laugh at yourself. Quite right. And then she told Friday a joke about me. If, she said, he only writes once every two weeks he must be short on ideas. I stayed silent. Not quite getting the point. Until Friday explained. Only write of the great and good. They are sparse. Lillian told us on leaving that she had prepared some cheese and chips but had forgotten. Preferred to gossip. We thought we had had a good deal.

We then went to see Pathri's four newly acquired buffaloes. Innovatively named One, Two, Three and Four. And two *bacchas*. Named immediately as Half and Half. The buffaloes, lying comfortably, groaned to their feet. Except for number One, who stared at me morosely, unmoved. With a regular diet, which they now receive, their milk yield has more than doubled. I was asked, solicitously, whether I liked buffalo. Only, I replied, honestly, between two slices of bread.

Meanwhile Friday had been chatting with the Gujjar ladies. This, for them, was a new experience. They are largely ignored by well wishers of Pathri during visits. Which is a shame! They have many excellent ideas for the advancement of themselves and their community which are probably ignored by the Village Eco Development Committee. The ladies have learnt to sew. They proudly displayed to us what they has stitched for themselves and their children. And are anxious to become self-sufficient. If they can receive more sewing machines with treadles, they can be.

Nellie, the elephant packed her trunk and said goodbye to the circus. So runs the old British musical song. In the case of one of our Rajaji National Park elephants this was not a wise decision. Doon was saddened by yet another elephant from Rajaji being struck by a train while treading the traditional elephant path which is unfortunately bisected by the railway track from Haridwar to Dehra Doon. This time the victim was a young calf. Its mother responded in true maternal fashion. No one could approach young Nellie. Our local state veterinary officer had been deployed in Delhi to supervise the welfare of the elephants participating in the Republic Day parade. In case one should tumble under a tank. The Mussoorie Express, carrying Governor Barnala, was forced to return to Haridwar. Having being charged by Nellie's irate mother. Nellie's mother and her entire family stood guard. She died. Requiescat in pace.

12

Flying Zone

In Doon it is still time for adventures before the avalanche of tourists arrive. There are some spots unknown to the invaders. The lake, where the night birds sing, although not quite like the nightingale in Grosvenor Square from where the songbirds have long fled under the illuminated eagle of their embassy. I recite, nostalgic from *Ode to a Nightingale*. 'Thou was not born for death immortal bird...' Poor Keats! We agreed to open the wine. Mother Ganga slides slowly, in no hurry to meet the burnt bodies at Benaras. Still rejoicing in her pristine purity before the horrors of the Hooghly, 'with dirty little coasters and salt-stained smoke stacks butting down the river in the mad monsoon with a cargo of Bihari coal, road rails, pig lead, baubles and cheap tin trays.' Sorry to bastardise Masefield. But he deserves it.

Another hospitable Doon family, the local *patwari* in Vikas Nagar, invited me to stay for a night, or longer. This was for my new territory in Uttaranchal. The approach through the suburbs was less than prepossessing. But the family were warm and caring. No meat, they apologised, as it was Navratri. No problem. The next morning we went on a bumpy tour to see where the river Tons emerged from its fifteen kilometer journey through a mountain tunnel to blend with the Jamuna near Daak Pathar and then to join in an impressive series of hydro-electric stations on the canal. The surplus water was diverted, but the main thrust was to the six power stations downstream. Once you have seen one power station, entry to which is denied without a press card, you have seen them all. They were identical, but doubtless pulsating electricity to Uttaranchal and other states. My host said that we must go to where the canal stopped. I forebode to explain that canals do not stop. So we discovered that this canal on its long journey again disgorged into another mountain and ended up in Meerut. So where, I asked myself, sitting by the riverside of the depleted Jumna did all the water go? Over to Chesterton, 'Noah often said to his wife when he sat down to dine, I don't care where the water goes if it doesn't get into the wine.'

In the sun, the pool fish are frisky and flirting. More eggs to hatch. I play the Brandenbergs which they seem to appreciate. Then Brahms. But Berlioz send them scurrying under the stones. It does the same for me. Except that I would not fit. The garden is a symphony of colours. Maali has learnt not to plant in straight lines, but to let blooms intertwine and colours complement each other. The Brandenbergs, like the conflict in Baghdad, rise to a crescendo. The TV server goes down. Saddam might well, but Bach will never.

It is time for construction on the small hill opposite my land. By now the ugly bricks are hidden behind flowers of flame of the forest trees. In the garden the silver oak trees are admired by the passers-by on the way to Mussoorie where some previously defunct hotels have been bought over by Delhi developers. Let us hope that like the owners of the Imperial Hotel, they make a better job than their predecessors. Mussoorie and Doon deserve it.

Flies. The bane of our lives. Especially in pre-monsoon Doon. Shoo them away and they come back for another attack. One after another. Insatiable. First the nose, then the ears, and they are remarkably agile. If one lands in your coffee, the desire to drink it evaporates. I have seen grown men in Doon chasing an elusive fly around the room. Perhaps they, the flies, don't watch television. But my guests, hand clapping, pursue. No spray works. The beauties lap it up. Strange, I never see any fly at Kalyani's. The flywhisk was invented in India, so they say, now sadly a plastic fly ridder is remarkably effective. After the swat, even if not successful, they stay clear. To pester someone else. But if you succeed in your first attempt, you can quote Oscar Wilde, 'Nothing to declare except my genius.' What sadistic delight! A fly in one.

13

Tully Ho! Ganga is in Gujrat

I love music, but prefer to listen rather than watch. This relates to an earlier experience in my diplomatic career. Posting at Budapest was both priceless and a pain. The telephones, tapped of course, were troubled by tardy tinkers, who went off for lunch between one and two. Then home to bed by eleven. No relief or shift workers. They just disconnected the telephone. This was a minor discomfiture. My main one was the ambassador. Now long fallen off the twig, he was known, especially to the Hungarian, as 'One drink M'. That is all you ever got. Sir M, whose wife was an Austrian countess, had high hopes of ending his career in Vienna. 'Sorry,' said the Foreign Office. 'Budapest is only a few hours drive.'

Sir M was an opera buff. His wife was not. In those days, the British ambassador had commandeered a private box in Budapest's finest opera house. He was supplied with a chaise lounge with a superb view of the stage. And screened from the audience by a low balcony. Wine and champagne offered. Sir M did not only like opera he thought he could sing it. Arias in a false soprano, contralto and bass were all within his range. The Hungarian opera was then pretty short of money. And would, quite frankly, take any musician who had a larynx, knew the tunes and had an evening dress. The operas were thus presented in a miscellany of European tongues varying from Romanian through Bulgaria, Czech, Russian and Italian to Hungarian. Sadly, my ambassador's fluent languages in song were German and Greek. But he was enthusiastic and determined to impress. Equipped with an operatic score, he would sing every piece in either language or both. From his box. Much to the consternation of those on stage. And to the increasing anger of the audience. I, on duty would sit on a higher chair in full view of the audience. And well away from the ambassador's refreshments. The audience and artists obviously attributed the awful noise to me. A junior diplomat's life is not a happy one.

A very sweet letter from, I suspect, a very young lady from Pune. She tells me Pune is into *The Asian Age*. And she added that Pune is full of really interesting people. Why don't I write about them? Replying sympathetically, I gently said that writing about Pune without visiting the city would be wrong. I could have said 'immoral', but they probably have not yet taught this to Class Four. I recall a BBC staffer dramatically reporting the tragic earthquake in Gujrat, while in Benares, saying, 'This is the BBC reporting from Ganga in Gujrat.' Not naturally, Mr Tully.

14

Sane Dog & Englishman: Why One Prefers Sandals, the Other, Ursula Andress

It was Friday, Sunday and I went for lunch, she promising me *idli* and *sambar* with coconut *chutney* which proved to be unavailable. Instead, we were offered sunk *tangri* followed by a 'green mean mint soup.' This was followed by 'drums of heaven' with sesame fingers and a chicken lollipop. And what meal would be complete without a *murg saagwala* translated into English as, 'raped in *murgh palak*'? One is left gasping for breath especially when one is served hot honeymoon chocolate fudge with tooty fruity on the side. I asked as an accompaniment to my meal, a Virgin Mary. Virgins they could supply, but a Mary was difficult.

A quiet if thirsty day in Doon. The first welcome, the second soon quenched. Initially with *dahi* and bananas, the brain assimilating the morning *akhbar* The telephone did not work, probably perspiring in the heat. But Jeeves expertly effected repairs to the system. Later, when it got stuck again, Sunday used her hair contraption to make it work. And work it did, and has since. I hope that BSNL are not reading this. They charge a fortune to send an engineer on a cycle and for another with a ladder, although telephone cables in Rajpur have been laid underground for a year.

I am under instructions from Girl Sunday and the staff to eat more. And to drink less. Everyone approves although their percentage from the liquor shop will diminish. On this Sunday, Jeeves, Freddy and I visited the Rajpur village Sunday market. There were firm capsicums, dying to be stuffed with spiced lamb mince and *pudina*, aubergine fried with cauliflower, cheese coated. White *muli* basked in balsam vinegar, spinach lightly sautéed with garlic. Freddy approved, although he didn't eat meat. Then returned to his milk and husk to chew a *chappal* while watching this odd Englishman enjoying an old James Bond movie: *Where is Ursula Andress?*

Breeder Mike Dalvi asked us for lunch in his farm, way far from the madding crowd in the forests before Selaqui. He nurtures a variety of animals and birds, not to mention his farm produce. There are grouse and pheasants, but not to be shot.

Other varieties of animals, and of course, his extensive range of trees. Sunday had a Virgin Mary while me and Mike had a convivial, if slightly boozy, lunch before touring his extensive home and farm. It was too much to take in for a day. A few hours is not enough amidst the sal forests. Such beauty and rural peace! Mike has asked us to spend more time to explore the farm. We left with Kalyani singing *Mama Mia* in supreme soprano while I sinking safely to sleep in the back seat.

15

Speeches, Mosquitoes and Other Things that Bite

I returned to Delhi from Doon with great reluctance but with a sense of duty for a family *shaadi*. I have attended many *shaadi* functions but it has been some time since I have been a participant in the full Monty. At a previous wedding, Punjabi style, the English bridegroom, soon to become a friend through sheer fright, watched fearsome Sikhs parading their *kirpans*. His English friends had wisely got lost in Rajasthan. He was naturally nervous. The Sikh warriors, dressed like warlords, waved their *kirpans* in the air, more with bravado than common sense. I asked the Englishman solicitously 'Have you been circumcised?' I thought he might faint from which I assumed that he hadn't. A few dozen Bloody Mary's later he was sprightly as a lamb and even tried to nick one of the Sardarji's swords.

This *shaadi* was more sober. It included my nephew. He was there because he was the bridegroom. Otherwise, he would have been quite superfluous. The function was to impress relatives and friends. Beautifully arranged, stage managed, the bride and groom were the lead actors in the *tamasha*. Dutifully playing their parts for the gratification of others. And they performed well, although their inner thoughts were an enigma. I asked my nephew before I thankfully left for the comfort of the Mussoorie Express to return to the civilisation of Doon, whether he had enjoyed the experience. 'Oh yes, David Uncle,' he replied, lurching, eyes glazed, to greet a new arrival whom he had never met before and would never meet again. No bedsprings twanging that night, I thought. Just the heavy breathing of their deep sleep of exhaustion in the honeymoon suite. What a waste!

I attended the 2001 Doon School Founders at the invitation of several of the members of the governing body. The school is considered one of India's most prestigious for boy's education. India's equivalent of Eton. Having heard old Etonian friends talk about their alma mater, I was eager to see if the same mysteries shrouded Doon. They did.

The chief guest this year was Mr Amitabh Bachchan, accompanied by the ubiquitous Amar Singh. Mr Bachchan's presence quite naturally created an enormous interest. So much so that for the first time many Doscos and their guests could not be accommodated in the Rose Bowl and sat outside, glumly, watching the proceedings on a large television screen. The identity of the chosen few in the Rose Bowl remains a mystery. Some *chamchas* of a political group?

The parents looked forward to a long, turgid and boring speech from the headmaster about their children's achievement. He did not disappoint. There were two incongruities. The first time was when Mr J. Mason described his boys as 'innocent souls'. Tell, that to the Welham Girls! The second was when a generous would-be benefactor sent a promissory note of ten lakhs in the middle of the headmaster's report, expecting, if not demanding, instant and public recognition from the school and the audience. He got it. Dosh over dignity.

Mr Bachchan, who was in severe pain with neck and lumbar troubles, manfully read out his speech saying in genuine bewilderment that he could not quite understand why he had been invited. He has, after all, never been invited as chief guest to his old school, Sherwood, Nainital. He nevertheless spoke feelingly to the attentive audience. Bollywood bilge delivered in the most rapturous and seductive style. The singer not the song.

By now the mosquitoes had begun to attack. In force. Decision time. Retreat to the safety of the mosquito free Upper

Rajpur Road or stay for the music. I elected to stay. It was a wise decision. The Doon boys performed magnificently. An original composition, composed and directed by Mr Gurcharan Singh. It was well worth the discomfiture, both from the insects and the interminable tuning of instruments. I felt sorry for Mr Mason. So many powerful old boys who think, once a year, that they can do a better job.

In contrast I went to the Welham Girls' Founders Day. There was no Amitabh Bachchan, no Dev Anand or even a Bollywood bird. It was superbly organised by the principal, Mrs J. Brar. Guests on arrival were greeted by polite, neatly clad Welham students who directed us to our seats. The ceremony was brief. The chief guest, Mrs Aruna Roy, spoke concisely and the principal's report was equally brief and to the point. It was followed by an audio-visual presentation created by the students. Brilliantly demonstrating the social work, voluntarily undertaken by the Welham Girls in addition to their curriculum. Miss Grace Mary Linell would have been proud.

They say, quite correctly, that a Welham Girl on her own is a delight. Two together are bearable. Just. Three or more and one must pray for some decent cricket on the television. All night.

In total contrast to the grand events at the founder's days of the Dehra Doon schools was a meeting of the Governing Council of Raphael. I am, proudly so, a newly elected member. General Bakshi chaired the meeting with military precision.

He outlined his sensible plans for the future and did not dwell on the past, estimable as it is. It was unnecessary to do so. We all knew of Raphael's achievements. So why, boringly restate them? Sir Rob Young, the British Commissioner has donated Rs 400,000 to Raphael. The Polish Embassy was astonished to learn the 'Little White House', the home and teaching establishments for the healthy children of cured lepers, was named by Lady Sue Ryder of Warsaw, from a Polish folk song which 'tells of a house where children entered and found happiness'. The spirit of the folk song is happily established in Lady Sue Ryder's Little White House in Dehra Doon. Lady Ryder was awarded five different orders of merit by the Polish government between 1965 and 1966. These included the Golden Order of Merit, the Polish Humanitarian Award and also, charmingly, in 1981, the Polish Order of the Smile.

In the war against the Nazis, Polish Airmen joined and fought valiantly with the British Royal Air Force. Polish ladies were wonderful nurses on the Allied Front. Raphael does not need fighter pilots. But it would be a significant gesture of friendship if Poland were to help in the training of nurses for Raphael.

On the way from Mussoorie to Dehra Doon, Girl Friday and I inadvertently got lost and stumbled upon a snake temple. We had no clue as to when it was constructed. There was no priest or guru to guide us. We could only speculate or dream;

the clouds swirling spectacularly then to show us the mountains above and the valley below. The snake temple contained shrines dedicated to various other Gods. Shiva, Radha-Krishna, Hanuman; Durga and Saraswati. Having entered the inner temple and made my *namaste* to the Snake God I felt that all the sanctum sanctorum, whatever your religion, are possessed with power; potential and powerful.

For live snakes Girl Friday and I went to see the snake village locally known as the Sapera Basti of Jhani Goan near Rajpur. The villagers were originally gypsies but had settled in the *basti* over forty years ago. The *basti* has now accepted the patronage of the Moravian Institute. Some villagers have conveniently converted to Christianity. More, I suspect for free bricks and mortar than a belief in Christ. The villagers' hearts remain with Kali. The only religious function celebrated by the villagers is Naag Panchami. Live snakes of all colours, shapes and sizes were presented for our delictation. But none were for sale. The villagers use snakes to bargain and exchange.

A python, a rat snake and two cobras were produced. The cobras, remembering the silver symbolic ones which I buried in my cottage foundation, were quite special. Revealing their sinister hoods, I plucked up courage and gingerly dropped a hundred rupee note into their baskets. Appeased, they subsided.

The snakes are caught by the villagers in the jungles of Doon by laying a small stick across their heads. Rampart rising cobras are charmed by music and mantras. The villagers do not remove the venom of the snake. If bitten there is a herbal remedy, which is quite expensive. Mantras matter more. And, we were told, as effective. In the absence of the Master of the Mantras, his son, Ramesh told us that snake catching and the knowledge of the mantras was a dying art. The senior snake charmer present, Lacchman Singh, accepted a cigarette. The snake village is not yet, thankfully designated as a 'public place'. Come again, said Mr Singh, for our snake festival. Girl Friday shuddered.

16

Why Insurance is Not My Policy

One of my first experiences of India was an aquatint by Thomas Daniell and his nephew William who portrayed India through their sketches. Earlier on, their pictures sold at a pittance. Now they are priceless. I was lucky in those days to buy a selection. Now Delhiwallahs spend lakhs of rupees to visit Christies and Sotheby's to claw back the treasures which England left to India. But apart from Daniell, there was a great lady painter, Emily Eden, whose sketches were few and rare. Her aquatints of the missing princes from the Aurangzeb era hang proudly on the walls of my cottage in the original wooden frames, although one is sequestered in London. The princes were murdered for loot, lustre and for kingship. The original owner, Annette Strover, in her 80s now, still plays elephant polo in Nepal. Britain loves India for its multi-racial society, although we are still proud of it. We are happy to be welcomed back as friends and nowhere more than in the valley of Doon.

There is a strange correlation between Westerners who find religion elusive and Buddhism which seems more attractive. Hinduism is harsher in that it demands more from its devotees. Buddhism demands little and is easy to embrace. In Hinduism, one cannot convert although one can adopt the Hindu way of life. But you will never get there, unless reborn in the next life. Sunday and I decided on a fuggy afternoon to visit the Songtsen Library, mysteriously situated across the valley from the cottage, where we were greeted courteously by Tashi. Of the two libraries in Dehra Doon, the IMA offers the principle delights in every sort of book from *The History of the Roman Empire* to *The Saints Come Marching In*. The Tibetan Library, a library for spiritual scholars, gives visitors a range of books on Buddhism, Hinduism and Christianity in many languages. It, as usual, was immaculate and its director and staff were more than welcoming in our pursuit of the academic opportunities in the libraries of the Himalayas.

While tourists trek up Rajpur Road, looking enviously at my laden mango trees, Maali, early one morning, plucked the lychees which were husked and destoned by his daughter to end up canned. The one-kilo tins, glistening, now repose in the kitchen waiting for me to slurp over Christmas. They will be joined by tins of mango slices fresh from the trees while the *lakdi* crackles and chestnuts pop. With Mozart playing in the background and the promise of rain, although not yet fulfilled, both suddenly thunder in perfect symphony.

Sitting in the dusk of Doon, in the pre-monsoon muggy season, I idly and briefly watched a CNN programme about the difficulties and benefits of an expatriate living overseas, especially in India. It was hilarious, if misleading. On joining the diplomatic service in 1960, I received a terse letter stating that, 'You may be required to serve in difficult and dangerous posts.' Not 'choose to' nor to 'agree to'. You did what you were bloody well told. I did a brief spell in Paris, where one of my many difficulties was avoiding the predatory embassy secretaries. In Turkey, where my boss described the beer as 'gnats' pee' and where water was delivered weekly in earthenware pitchers, on a donkey cart. In Nigeria, where I bribed the heavily armed guards of the police chief next door to return my errant golf balls. They took a case of Guinness beer a week. Unlike India, in May serving dinner by candlelight, as there was no *bijlee*. Seychelles was where the many dangers were. A donation of the clap from the ladies. Hungary, with its then obsessive communist security Aparat, was illuminating as were the men who obsessively chased me around the country having free meals in every restaurant, doubtless having inserted a microphone into the pretty rose bowl on the table. In London my then grilfriend, Meg, and her mother announced that I could work for the Prudential Insurance Company, processing policies. No way. Yes, she married the man from Prudential. And they take the same train to work every day. Swap stories about insurance claims over their sandwiches. By the edge of the sludgy Thames. And annually get lightly brown in southern Spain waiting for their demise in Golder's Green. Their knowledge of a dangerous place to visit is limited to a Bengali takeaway. What a waste!

Before leaving Dehra Doon and then for London, I was waitlisted No. 61 on the Shatabdi. Then over the last few days reduced to a confirmed ticket. It was a relief because the road journey is now becoming increasingly hazardous with the ravaging tourists returning with their spoils from the hills leaving behind them a sizeable amount of loot. They can afford it. Uttaranchal welcomes it, but not the trash they leave behind. Luckily, the boarding schools are closed for the summer and are thus spared this ignominy.

The monsoon in Doon is of considerable importance. And with its onset, the trees greening while the colours of the mountains subtly change, encased by a cloud, we sit and sip. We sip and sit while waiting for the *devis* and *devtas* to march down from the mountains. What joy! What thrills! What delight! For us and the plants and the trees in the garden to be inundated by rain fresh from the Himalayas. In the valley, some of the roofs will leak, especially those covered with rusty old tins. Mine have survived for two years with Mangalore tiles that have so far proved impermeable. I keep my fingers crossed. They say that the monsoon in Rajpur is more ferocious than many in Assam, but it is certainly joyous.

17

Sunny Sundays and Miserable Mondays

There is magic in the Ganga. My third encounter was at the Glass House above Rishikesh. Built again by the former Maharaja of Tehri, who seemed to have a fixation about building palaces. The Glass House, formally the Maharaja's hunting lodge, is now a heritage hotel managed by Francis Waziarg and Amar Nath. Here Ganga flows paradoxically north before joining its natural southern and eastern flow. Ganga was mountain green. Rocks creating white froth disturbed only by the occasional river rafter. There is something magical about waking to the sound of running water. And I don't mean a leaky loo. Next door to the Glass House is Mani Thapar's estate. Also on the Ganga. I dropped in for a dip. Ganga seemed more reflective. Perhaps convinced, finally, of my sincerity.

In school, as a boy, we were taught how to write letters. Is this a dying art? The e-mail, voice-mail and fax are replacing the letter. But with what anticipation one looks at an envelope, a real one, delivered by a live postman. Even to see the stamps. To look at the postmark. It conjures hopes, expectations and fears about its content. To guess, or to wish? Then to read. It is not hopefully, the bank statement.

Most middle-class Indian families agonise over their children's education. Parental pressures to achieve results often lead to disappointment. In Britain, among the richer and middle-classes, the view used to be more relaxed. Not anymore. Daddy and Mummy's school no longer have open doors for their sons and daughters as in India, where fees and donations put many schools out of reach. My son failed marginally, his Eton examination. He was subsequently happy in King's Canterbury, where he acquired, from visits to his *baniya* grandfather, 'business.'

In King's wing collars were derigueur. They cost one and half pounds each. The boys also wore black morning suits. The enterprising lads would parade around Canterbury Cathedral, where the school was housed in its grounds. Shamelessly posing in uniforms for photographs by American and Japanese tourists. For a pound. Then sell their wing collars for two. Boarding school is perhaps an institution peculiar to England and India; maybe in the subcontinent. Society in Italy and

France frown. Children sent away, they feel, must be either deprived or demented. Sandeep Dutt from Doon, a writer and researcher on education, has written ten books on the subject both in Doon (his latest revision published this year) and one on other schools in India. No plugs. The books are objective, not as the author says, subjective and better for it. In the end it must be the parent and the child's choice. The greatest gift to give to your child after home care is education.

The libraries in the Indian Military Academy are treasure houses. I spent another wintry day browsing through leather-bound photographic records, this time of the Amateur Dramatic Club, 1946-1948. The IMA Ladies Dramatic production of Tagore's *Chitman* produced by Lalita Talibuddin, directed by Amar Chatterjee. In 1948 there was a competition. One company presented the *Boatswain's Mate*. By W.W. Jacles, *The Casino Company*, *The Death Trap* followed by Charles Wright's *Check Mate* and *Shivering Shocks* by Clement Dane. There is no record of who won. The cast and directors were a healthy mixture of Indian and British. With a strange Italian prisoner of war thrown in for an Aria. The jewel in the crown was Sheridan's *The Scheming Lieutenant* starring K.K. Mehra, Ajit Prasad and Esme Russell. Does India have a Justice Credulous?

It is Sunday morning, sunny. Maybe spring has sprung. The plants think so. The garden is blooming and blossoming. Mali and Miss Mali, his young daughter, enter the cottage, silently, to tend to the indoor plants. Mali sagaciously tests the soil. And filches filtered water for his favourites. Miss Mali cleans the leaves of dust. Satisfied, they slip away. Mali to the vegetable garden, where he wills the carrots to plumpen. Miss Mali to her classes at school.

Onto a miserable Monday, Doon drenched. Spring forgotten. And after some pointed hints from friends, I decided it was time for a haircut. My barber has a small stall in Rajpur village. He clipped and clopped. Rain drummed. Predictably the *bijli* vanished. Barber kept cutting. Aided by his newly acquired daughter-in-law holding a candle, he seemed to know what he was doing. It was only when he began sharpening his razor, that I began to have doubts. But all went well. Not a nick. Except nicked for twenty rupees. Perhaps Uttaranchal might invite foreign tourists for the unusual experience of a haircut and shave by the light of a candle. There is no charge for the candle.

18

Chutney Roads and Ruskin's Advice

The PWD and the wizards from the water department have dug up Chakrata Road in Dehra Doon. The main thoroughfare from the clock tower to all places south. The reason is to lay new water pipes. And with foresight, sewage pipes. What goes in, must come out. The pipes will be laid adjacent to each other, forever locked in embrace but not bolted. Ugh! 'And why down the middle of the road?' I asked. 'On the sides there are shops and stalls. We would encroach,' was the answer. 'But these shops themselves are encroachments, hiding some of the once lovely Muslim architecture and *havelis* in old Doon,' said I. The answer: 'We are a middle of the road government. Centrist.' Never challenge an expert on his own ground, however shaky the foundations. Now to demonstrate the point, an English pop song of the fifties:

There he was, digging this hole
Hole in the ground big and sort of round it was
When along comes a Babu with his big clothe cap
Hey you, he said, you can just stop that
You're digging it round and it ought to be square
And not in this place so dig it elsewhere
The ground's now levelled and completely flat
And beneath it is the Babu and his big cloth hat

The New Year brings good news to Raphael with the very substantial donation of funds by retired Wing Commander Barney Fernandez who lives in Australia. So much of the continuing donation to the Raphael Cheshire Homes comes from countries in the Pacific rim, notably Australia and New Zealand. Barney Fernandez after his retirement from the Indian Air Force in 1996 has raised three academy's to train pilots in South East Asia and Africa. He will be visiting India early this month and we intend to give a warm Doon welcome. Most of the funds come from retired members of the Indian armed forces who remember Raphael with affection and the work done by Genral Bakshi.

Friends in London established a restaurant called 'Chutney Mary's' in fashionable Chelsea near the football club. The menu based on Anglo Indian cuisine hails originally from those railway stations invariably beginning with an English name and ending in Gunj. It was here, where generations of Anglo Indians worked on railways, created their own societies and their own cuisine. Chutney Mary is hugely successful in London although, I regret to say that I did not like the food. Too much chutney and not enough Mary. I sat next to Shobha De and neither the Bloody Marys (not enough vodka) and the rims of the glasses thickly incrusted in salt made for a companionable meal.

It was therefore with some apprehension that I accepted an invitation to lunch in Barlowgunj at Skinner Hall; not because I had any qualms about their company which is perennially delightful, but as Lillian told me in advance that their Sunday lunch was invariably Anglo Indian food. Lillian presided with Sylvia. One of the brothers, Jim, had been badly injured in a motor accident. Now fast recovering although still on a walker, we exchanged pleasantries on hip replacements, fractured vertebrae and a badly bent knee. I only wish that I had done something to my coccyx. Only because like the American expression, 'The opera ain't over till the fat lady sings,' I have never found an opportunity to use either the fat lady or a coccyx in any of my articles. So another ambition was achieved.

Lunch was delicious, unpretentious and wholesome. Old stories of the Skinner families emerged with different dishes.

There was Aunty Alice who passed away in 1923. A savvy lady who had accumulated large tracts of land. She was a formidable dame. And built a brewery for the thirsty British troops en route by foot to the Mussoorie Garrison. Tales of the Skinner dynasty which went from clog to clog in five generations. Aunt Alice would turn in her grave probably shattering mountains with rage, but the lovely Skinners are not bitter, for they live life to the full and enjoy it. I opened a bottle of wine with a corkscrew surely dating from the eighteenth century. It had a bone handle and a twist of metal for the cork. The Skinner ladies looked apprehensively as I manipulated this machine. A collective sigh of relief when the cork went pop and the contents were enjoyed by one and all sitting in front of a *bukhara* as snowflakes gently began to fall.

Earlier in Sisters Bazaar, I had called on Ruskin Bond who kindly descended from his apartment on lethal steps which, I thought, I could not ascend. He was right. He presented me a copy of his latest book. *The Rupa Book of Nightmare Tales.* We sat overlooking the valley huddled in our respective winter clothing. I asked for advice on writing a book. Keep it short, he said, thirty to forty thousand words. Anyone, who goes on longer, gets boring. Advice, which I will take to heart. The wind chill factor soon drove me to the comfort of the Qualis and Ruskin to his warm home with invitations for future chats, possibly over an Old Monk or two at the Savoy Hotel.

With Dussehra and Diwali approaching, it is open season in Doon for the begging bowl. I have some sympathy for youths who wash car windows for a modest sum. But none for those with well nourished bodies demanding money for doing nothing. And would sell their sisters for a shilling. Three such arrived at my cottage with a pamphlet printed badly in Hindi inviting me to come to a Diwali function and give a large donation. The pamphlet was passed to Sunday for translation and advice. She in turn slipped it over to Jeeves. One glance and both agreed that it was not going to happen. Sunday consulted Freddie who gladly came up with a solution. He sniffed; grabbed and went silently to a corner ripping it into tiny snowflakes.

There is in Doon, whom our local newspaper describes as 'he or she is an iconoclast, a breaker of idols in theory if not in practice'. I looked the word up in the dictionary. It sanctimoniously and appropriately means an extinct marine mammal dedicated by the Greeks to the worship of Idolatory, the deification of images. It's all Greek to me said Sunday wisely. Take your pick and return to the realism of 2003.

19

If Love is Novel,
International Love is a Fiction

Scouting through the Dehra Doon telephone directory in search of a printer, I came across an entry for Princess Rajendra of Limbi. I was intrigued and telephoned, more in hope than in expectation. I introduced myself to her daughter, Mrs Shamsher Singh, and asked for an interview. Nothing ventured, nothing gained. Two days later, I was asked for drinks at the home of the princess in her impressive house above Rajpur village. Lt General (Retd.) Shamsher Singh joined us for a convivial *bada* peg. Then the princess, looking frail but interesting, joined us. She spoke perfect English. It would have been rude to ask her age or even guess it. Originally from Punjab, Kalshia and from Saurashtra, now Gujrat, her mother was the Maharani of Kalshia. The princess met a man on a steamboat on the way to England and a love match ensued. A cricket enthusiast, the family produced the vice-captain of the first Indian Test team to visit England. He was a tennis blue at Cambridge University. His name was Gham Singham Singh. I had expected a short interview, but we sat companionably for two hours. Me with Old Monk and the princess slowly sipping a glass of Goan port. I promised that I would bring some stuff from London. And did. Coburns vintage.

A day of swings and roundabouts for us Doon Dodos. A visit to Ruskin Bond who signed his latest anthology of British writers of ghost stories. H.W. Dennys, Gerald T. Tait and of course, Colonel Sleeman who wrote in 1844 about haunted villages; Alice Perrin who wrote of the summoning of Arnold. Ruskin is best described as a friendly writer especially for children. He inscribed the book, 'May you find a few friendly ghosts down in Rajpur!' And in Girl Sunday's copy, 'Best of luck in your journalistic endeavours!' Then Sunday and I took Lillian Skinner for lunch. As usual, she sparkled and confessed that her birthday would be in September, her eightieth. This would be a great event, an occasion for a *burra* bash. Kalyani has offered to cook. Driving down to Doon, I remarked that Lillian looks much younger than her age. 'Younger than you do,' said Sunday. Thanks! Back to Bloody Marys.

A chance meeting in Doon with an American boy and girl in India to 'do good.' It made them, they told me seriously, 'feel good.' And they were doing good with the poor. But they said, bitterly, their efforts were not widely appreciated, despite their contributions in cash and kind. How to explain to these innocents that the recipients of advice and aid often feel humiliated and patronised? *I've been working all day* sang Cat Stevens, now a converted Muslim. So now the Americans go to a five-star hotel to congratulate themselves over dinner. I end with a quotation from the notable American diplomat, Charles Thayer: 'International love is a fiction, the search of which has frequently ended in embittered frustration, particularly among Americans, whose passion for popularity is seldom understood.'

I received a very friendly letter from a brigadier at the Indian Military Academy who had been posted to Kargil. By coincidence, the Kargil conflict was over, or at least on hold. So he was posted to Jalandhar. A visit to him is in the diary. I have never visited Kargil, but do have less than lovely memories of Jalandhar. Most probably the cantonment, as usual with military establishments, will reveal a more presentable portrait. I was in Jalandhar to buy cricket bats. One of my foolish ventures in the family export business. Their attempt to keep me away from the fleshpots of the British diplomatic service. Fat chance! I bought the cricket bats. For the

Madagascar police force. But no pads or boxes were ordered. Not needed, they said. Stout chaps. I later learned that no cricket was ever played in Madagascar. So I returned salutarily to the relative sanctity of the Foreign Service, where torture is administered by the pen and not by the bat. In those days, the Foreign Office agreed or rejected approvals for export licences, in particular for arms and other items of military requisition. A young colleague was on the Argentine desk; in those days it was a repressive military regime. She told me proudly over a lunch-time beer that she had signed an approval for the export of two hundred silenced Sterling submachine guns for the Argentine prison service. 'They need them,' she said. 'So as not to disturb the local residents.' The last I heard, she works in the Foreign Office's reference library.

'God is love,' I said to Sunday. 'You,' she announced with accuracy, 'are not God, at least not mine.' It was one of those spiritual days with Kalyani spending Sunday meditating and if I had intruded, I would have received one of her 'looks.' She says that God does not like repeated prayers without 'Ump.' So she went diverse. Now the whole neighbourhood wakes up to her spiritual gong. Here is the interesting part. She does not know when she is going to do it. She just does it. Thank God, that she lives far away.

20

LEG–Break: Bad Dog and Englishman

Before the Doon winter chills it was time to revisit a secret and secluded spot on the Ganga. The water level is low so I could safely swim, or rather paddle across accompanied by Freddie. Our objective was to inspect two forest bungalows with the purpose of acquiring one, with supreme views of Mother Ganga and the mountain. Both bungalows sufficiently dilapidated to deter all but the most foolhardy. There is no access by road. Only by boat across the Ganga.

Dogs, lovable animals, until Freddie, now old enough to freely roam the garden, welcomed me back to the cottage, by jumping on my shoulders. He is now fifteen kilograms. And catapulted me on the concrete. Then, abashed, he retreated to his quarter. Jeeves applied liniment and a sleeping pill. Next morning he inspected my right knee. I could not walk. After breakfast Jeeves announced 'hospital.' He and the Maali shoved me into the Qualis to meet Dr Rajneesh Singh at Disha Hospital. He knew what to do. The X-Ray confirmed my fears. A fractured kneecap. It could have been worse said Rajneesh Singh. At your age a broken leg or a hip bone was common in England. You need metal pins in the knee. A local anaesthetic? I asked hopefully. A friendly, if pitying, look told me otherwise. We must slit you open. Better go to bye-byes. But in the meantime a small operation to extract blood from the knee to release pressure. Suck out the blood. Jeeves and Maali watched attentively, storing up stories with which to entertain their friends over *khana*. It took only two hours and didn't hurt—much. Do you want the blood, asked Rajneesh. Do I look like Dracula? Dr Singh laughed, but the needle went unerringly to its destination. My leg was bound in a plaster but I could wiggle my toes. The doctor, a sound man, offered a painkiller. He was sympathetic when I proposed him a gin and tonic. He advised *kurta* and shorts. What my thirty dinner guests that evening will think, I can only imagine, but failed to care. Sunday has resigned again in exasperation. But neighbour Jagdish has sent one of those quaint little artifacts found in hospitals for patients peeing in bed. Jeeves laughed all the way to the loo.

This is a tale about a dog and a leg. The dog is Freddie. The leg is mine. As usual I take on a minor role staying in the winds.

On a stretcher. To be as humorous as possible in the circumstances, rather like the banana skin joke. One mans' misfortune produces gales of laughter from others. To the party. Guy Fawkes' night on 5 November is the anniversary of the infamous gunpowder plot when a group of dissidents attempted to blow up the British Houses of Parliament. Sadly, many believe, they failed, were caught and paid the ultimate penalty. Three hundred years later the Indian Lok Sabha nearly suffered the same fate, with, happily, the same outcome. But Guy Fawkes' night in England is celebrated with children building bonfires and, for weeks before, asking for money displaying cloth replicas of Guy Fawkes to burn on a bonfire, eat sweet cakes, roast chestnuts, let off fireworks and be merry. And eat that curious Welsh pudding made from honey with ground gram and nuts. Well, the Welsh are all nuts. So, as Sunday tells me am I. I livened up Doon with a Guy Fawkes' night. *Patakas* authorised by the police until eight pm. A bonfire, roast jacket potatoes with lashings of butter and herbs. Pizzas, chicken wings and salad. Plumcake with red currant jam and custard cream. Fruits and cheese. I doubt Guy Fawkes received such a repast on his last evening on earth, although the surviving members of the House of Commons undoubtedly did. Sujeet Das, Secretary, home revenue and prisons, and his wife and their sweet daughter arrived. Was she, I asked, afraid of *patakas?* The non-noisy variety? Her answer was negative. Freddie was anxiously, and in wonder, curled in front of the bonfire on a chilly evening chewing contentedly on *singara*. Soon time for bed, he yawned. Freddie, not the Das' delightful young daughter.

It was with some trepidation that I arrived in Delhi and went into the arms of Sir Ganga Ram Hospital. I was surrounded by doctors of all shapes and disciplines. The most important is Dr (Mrs) Sood who is the chief anesthetist. No problem she said, we will give you an epidermal. A simple injection into the spine, if we can find it, and you will be paralysed from the waist down. Not permanently, I whispered and she giggled. But why not a general? I told her that one can rationalise with rum, get frisky with whisky, get randy with brandy, but sleep by general anaesthetic is not on my short list of treats. The fateful day arrived and I was stretchered to the Ganga Ram operating wing. The epidermal delivered by the good Dr Sood was painless. I soon lost all feelings below the waist. I looked in vain for a pretty nurse. A tall turbaned Sardarji doctor, Dr Maini, the leading expert in his field, asked how I felt. 'Bloody scared,' I told him truthfully. 'How much longer?' 'We just finished,' he said. 'so now go back to bed.' Not everybody is as lucky or privileged as I. There is inevitably overcrowding. But it was the cheerfulness and dedication which impressed me. The British National Health Service has something to learn. Readers might like to know that Sir Ganga

Ram, who inaugurated the hospital, was a wealthy philanthropist. His son-in-law Bharanvirji, governor of Punjab and West Bengal endowed the hospital with a state-of-the-art heart wing, I thank them and wish them well wherever they may be and of course the staff of Ganga Ram in the present day. One thing is missing. They don't teach docs to push wheel chairs.

Toothpick award of the month goes to MTNL. 'This number does not exist'. How many times have we received this pre-recorded message? The lady with the message in all probability does not exist, but some computer deep in the nether region of MTNL generates it. Does she exist? I ask. Do I? As with a friend of mine with whom I have spoken less than five minutes earlier and met a few minutes later for drinks at the India International Centre. 'Did you know,' I asked 'that you do not exist?' 'So I have been told.' he said, kindly signing the bill. 'I get the same message from my wife.'

21

Simply Foul, Neither Fish Nor Fowl

In Delhi, it is now mandatory for the passengers and driver of a vehicle to wear safetybelts. Conversely, in Dehra Doon scooter drivers are supposed to wear helmets, although, perversely, their passengers are not. This is enforced in Delhi, but sadly in Doon, the rule about helmets has been forgotten both by the riders and the police. For what reason, I do not know. But, the swirling dervishes of kids on motorcycles can still dent your car.

Yet another interesting couple in the valley of Doon. A Dr Dhirendra and Mrs Sharma, Director for the Centre of Science Policy Research. They live on their own in some seclusion in Bhagwantpur, fiendishly difficult to find for the first time, but eminently rewarding. Dr Sharma's centre specialises in scientific educational books translated into a variety of languages, aimed at bringing together young potential scientists in India. It is not an NGO and is funded by the Sharma's own resources. Dr Sharma is a sprightly seventy-five years of age who takes his British wife for an hour-long hike up the mountains near Mussoorie. Known locally as 'uncle', he offers food and employment to the villagers. Mrs Sharma teaches the local children for free. She takes brighter students from the neighbouring John Martin School and has succeeded in putting some of them into Scholar's Home where they perform as well as the children of the urban rich. Dr Sharma tells that one day he saw local children slipping and sliding across the local stream on the way to school. 'Why don't they build a bridge?' said his wife. 'Why don't we?' he said. And so they did, on their own without any financial support of their neighbours and the State authorities. Now the children and their mothers cross in safety as do the rich neighbours.

I dropped into the church of St John on the Rajpur Road, but apart from admiring the crumbling architecture and façade, I could feel little but sadness. Having felt thoroughly and rightly humbled by sharing space in *The Asian Age* with the Cardinal of Westminster on Christmas Day, I knew that I would never be a true Christian. The cardinal writes well, no very well. I am just not convinced. With advancing age, one turns hopefully to God or more often to cynicism. I fall into neither category.

Kalyani says that there has to be a special category for me. Neither fish nor fowl. But if God created us in his image as the Bible tells us, why are so many of us such bastards? Well, true conversion is unassailable. I remember, as a young Sunday school teacher, believe it or not, in St Jude's of Hampshire, telling my students not to genuflect. Moses and the graven image, if you remember. I tried introducing my charges to 'Honest to God' by the then Bishop of Woolwich. He said there is no heaven above and no hell beneath. He was reiterating the views of Dictrich Bonhoeffer, tortured paradoxically by the Nazis. Our church warden castigating Woolwich, drew on his own faith, belief and personal satisfaction which all gave him. Luckily, I had sufficient sense to refrain from telling him that he was preaching balls. Why, when a man is secure in his belief and content, should I pass scorn? Unkind, unfair and unchristian. The last in the true sense of the description.

Snoozing over the cricket on telly, I realised that there was a hot panting breath in my nostrils and someone was licking my knee. Accompanied by a large furry restless body. 'Could it,' I wondered, 'be the new masseuse?' A few more licks from a pink tongue established that it was not the lady with the oil and other lubricants. Freddie, who has no interest in cricket, decided to join me on the sofa. Although, how he got into the cottage is an enigma. He looked at me anxiously while emitting a contended smile, and as an Australian was caught behind, relapsed into slumber. Paws, wrapped around each other in fetal position in front of the log fire. I later found that he had wolfed my jam toast leaving the orange juice for me.

Spring in Doon has yet to begin, although, the brilliant sunshine and daily warmth tend to belie this. The spring bulbs, who should know better, are already sprouting with precocious optimism. Here in the garden, are, to quote Keats, 'sweet peas on tip toe for a flight.' Deep purple and raring to go. The Maharani of Jind from Mussoorie told me gloomily that the worst was yet to come. You have heard of the Indian summer, but this is the false Doon winter. The gods have yet to finish with us. So I stock up on *lakdee* and wait for the worst. Next week, Sunday and I will renew our friendship in Mussoorie and Barlowganj. And perhaps, stop at the Savoy Hotel for a beer and a view of the snow clad Banderpunch and with a bit of luck (*sic!*) catch a glimpse of our favourite ghost.

Another first time trip was to K.K.M. Hand Weaving, a registered society for the manufacturing and marketing of textile products by cured leprosy patients. Interestingly, almost all their products are exported to Germany and other European countries. It is one of five such mini villages that rely for their livelihood on their skills of spinning on a wheel—a replica of that used by Gandhiji—dyeing and weaving. This is another example of a minority who had previously no hope in life, having been shunned by their own people and society. They rather live in dignity than beg on the streets. Naturally, they were selling their products at prices which would make the Cottage Industries in Delhi bow their heads in shame. Sunday bought a few tablecloths and napkins.

In our eventually, successful attempts to find the Sharma household, we passed the deer park. Several times. I could see no deer although Kalyani and Jeeves saw more than one. I saw lots of monkeys and espied what I thought was a pelican. So to Dixon Lanier who wrote in the nineteenth century.

Oh a wondrous bird is the Pelican
His beak holds more than his belly can
He takes in his beak food enough for a week
But I am damned if I know how to the hell he can.

22

Why I Want a Slice of Turkey with Olives from Greece

It is, I said to Girl Monday when we began working together over a year ago, the ability to laugh at ourselves and not just to ridicule others that matters. We compromised. Now Monday and Freddy both laugh at me. I grin at the goldfish. At the tail end of the monsoon in Doon when the richer residents are returning from overseas trip, Sir Rob and Lady Young paid the valley what will certainly be their final trip to Doon before retirement. It was a welcome visit because in a modest way they have done a lot for institutions in the Doon Valley. A sizeable donation from the high commissioner's personal funds to Cheshire Homes.

When ambassadors, or in the case of India, high commissioners, retire, it is customary for them to write a valedictory despatch, covering their career and their last posting. These are confidential and are released to the public domain twenty-five years later when the persona and the authors are kicking up the daisies. Not, I hope, Rob Young. Nor would I expect this gentleman to write platitudinous or pompous prose. With his usual gentle wit on his farewell visit to Dehra Doon he left me with a ditty, dictated and composed in his car.

There was a good fellow called Keeling
Whose manners were very appealing
He invited to dinner
A Turner prize winner
And got him to paint on his ceiling.

Rob and Catherine retire all too soon to their place in France. So I riposte to their limerick with a piece of doggerel. Nicked from an old film by Mel Brooks. Plagiarised, but suitably amended for retirement:

All I want is peace. A little piece of Luxembourg to house
or bank account. Some bigger bit of Belgium for chocolates
just by chance. A larger slice of Turkey with olives from the
Greeks. Then our quiet place in France to frolic and to dance.

Sur Le pont D'Avignon. God speed. You're both unanimously elected honorary Loony Doonies.

We have had in India some disastrous appointments as High Commissioners. The late Sir Oliver Forster, who was Minister in my time and went on to be Ambassador in Pakistan, was a notable exception. In Delhi, he knew the names of every man, woman and child whether UK based or Indian staff at all levels in the mission. He, like the Chetwode statement, adhered to the principle that your country is first, your men are second, and you are third. Rob and Catherine have carried on this tradition and let us hope that his successor will emulate him.

I dropped in to my next door neighbour, Jagdish Prasad for a pre-prandial gin and tonic and to discuss the affairs of Rajpur Road. A large and ugly construction is facing him across the cud although the single brick work hardly a guarantee of longevity. Across from me the Delhites are pretentiously building a mansion which, I hope, the greenery of the trees will hide. If their servants don't cut them down. On a rainy day in Doon, I took Vichitri and Kalyani to lunch at Dev Dar Lodge, but first we went to call on Ruskin Bond who regaled us with tales worthy of a book. He gently laughed off my fanciful idea of being planted in the upper Landour cemetery. It was full he told me, but I might get a plot in the one on the other side of the road where they traditionally interred Roman Catholics. If I was not keen to spend my days with some mad Irish, I would do better to go to Camel's Back. There the owners, or possibly proprietors, were quite keen to sell plots. Ruskin has been offered one, but still feels unable to fall off the twig. I quite fancy my ashes being laid to rest on Camel's Back.

The Raphael Homes for the disabled recently held their annual general meeting for council members. This is normally brief. Supervised by nonagenarian General Bakshi. On this occasion, council members decided to raise questions about the audited accounts. Having difficulty in planning their own household arrangements the queries about expenditure on local cloth and footwear which continued interminably was a breath taking bore. I was disturbed from meditation, for which read snoozing, by the realisation that I was late for lunch. I hastily telephoned N.K. Singh, the Home Secretary to apologise for my tardiness. Mr Singh, unusually for a State Civil Servant, had assembled an interesting range of guests. We were all slightly taken aback to meet the new Director General of Police, Mrs Bhattacharya, who with her two daughters both studying in Canada, were less than menacing. It was a good lunch in a house which N.K. Singh supervised brick by brick taking him eighteen years. Not helped by the P.W.D. His wife who joins him from Delhi shortly will provide a welcome addition to the Doon society.

In Britain, in the great wars, any male civilian not in uniform would by happenstance be greeted by an irate female offering him a white feather. This was a symbol of cowardice, which was unfair, as most of those in civilian clothes were working in government offices and helping the war effort. Churchill praised them as handsomely as he did the fighting forces. The Raphael and Leonard Cheshire homes have revived the tradition of a red feather, a symbol of prosperity, security and happiness in the east. Many people now wear emblems denoting their commitment to gays, AIDS, and anything you like. But to wear a red feather singles you out as none of these, but a little bit kooky friend of the Cheshire homes. Mind you, the *maitre d'* of the Maurya might sniff and let you in. Alternatively, he might welcome you with a hug and a kiss.

23

If I Sing a Song, the Cows Will Go Home

Four Weddings and a Funeral was the title of a famous Hollywood movie. In Doon, the wedding season is drawing to an end. But we still have a fair number of funerals. The latest being of the renowned Hindi authoress Gaur Pant 'Shivani' who passed away recently. She spent many years in Almora and Kumaon in the Himalayas. Shivani recollected in her book, the long winter evenings when the family sitting next to the fire would huddle around the *saggar*. Dharam Viraji, who also passed away sometime ago, reminisced about his posting with the ICS as district collector in Almora. There, he said, he had more power and money than when he was cabinet secretary in Delhi. There were two syces to take care of his ponies. A host of servants, who would travel ahead on his tours of the district, set up his tents and ensure the correct temperature of his imported wine. I remember him sitting sparsely, the usual rose in his buttonhole and the pre-lunch gin and lime cordial and soda in his frail hand. Although a devout Hindu, following his wife's death, he became friendly with a *begum* from Hyderabad who introduced him to Muslim food. After the drinks he would sit down to a delicious *biryani, keema* and *pudina* sauce prepared by his Muslim *khansama*.

The Indian Military Academy in Doon under the command of Lt General Shergill is imbuing gentlemen cadets with Indian culture. This summer will see a joint exercise, no secret, between the IMA and the Bharatiya Kala Kendra. The operation, organised by Sumitra Charatram and Mrs Shergill, will present two Indian plays and ballets at the Academy auditorium and a separate performance for the students of local schools. Full marks to Gauri Keeling for setting this up. And to Girl Sunday for her organisational skills.

Sunday and I went to Sisters Bazaar where she spent most of her salary on cheese and dozens of other locally made delicacies. Mr Kumar, looking at me sympathetically, ensconced me in an easy chair. It was free so why should he care; but at least he bothered. So, in gratitude, I bought some Clouds End Honey. Mixed with Old Monk, it could provide competition to the classic remedy prescribed by Lily the Pink. On the way down from Sisters Bazaar, I bought white and pale gladioli. For a song. Sunday sang, quite prettily. Any sonorous soliloquy by me would have left the Gods of the Himalayas in a very bad mood. My father told me at a very early age, my singing voice would leave our cows constipated.

Summer is early in Doon. Jeeves has discarded his sweater, Master Jeeves peeks curiously at Sunday and her niece. Looks inquiringly through the window at them consuming pizza on a Saturday afternoon. I still wear a sweater. 'Never cast a clout till May be out,' was Aunt Annie's maxim. But she didn't live in India. Maali tramps through the garden without *chappals* and Miss Maali has her *chunni* wrapped securely around her neck. Aunt Annie was right. Sudden, abrupt and fierce rain swept the valley. I will, I told Sunday, shortly revert to my shorts. Don't, she advised. 'You look more presentable in light linen trousers.' I had always thought that I had attractive legs. No longer. So I duly bought some long legged trousers in Delhi.

Raphael Homes in Doon summoned me to the inauguration of a regional workshop on the promotion of Disability Rehabilitation by the Governor Sudarshan Agarwal, organised by the redoubtable General Bakshi, MC (Retd) and presided by Major Ahluwalia, PB of Everest fame, with Brigadier Sinha in attendance. It is surely a sign of a healthy society when so many retired military officers in India continue, in different ways, to serve their country. The governor, noted for his humanitarian consideration, gave a moving and at times passionate speech on the theme of the disabled needing a helping hand. He told a story of the young boy on the beach who would return stranded fish to the safety of the sea. When asked by an aged man passing by what good this did when there were so many hundreds of fish stranded after the high tide every day, the little boy replied that every fish he managed to pick up had a new chance in life. The governor's other strong message was that the attitude of society towards physical disability and not the disabled themselves must change to allow the former with the latter to become willing and useful members of the Indian nation. His sincerity was not in doubt. Let us hope that it is matched by his audience.

A girlfriend from yesteryear telephoned from Mumbai. She has a new boyfriend. Should she marry him? 'Has,' I asked 'he proposed?' 'He better,' she replied. Out of curiosity I enquired whether he was older than I. 'That,' said my Bengali bird, 'would be improbable if not impossible.'

24

How to Slip a Sloop into the Bottle

Girl Sunday asked me over for tea on predictably, a Sunday afternoon. With her happy-go-lucky plump sister in tow. I ended up drinking fairly respectable French white wine while Jeeves guzzled *pakoras* and *chai* that Kalyani had made especially for him. The previous afternoon, a beady character from Rishikesh whom I had met briefly in the past, had joined us after lunch and earnestly desired to write articles for newspapers. Did he have talent, he enquired. I could see from Girl Sunday's facial expressions that she was distinctly less than impressed. I could not but agree. It was a still and sultry afternoon with the prospect of dinner at the President Hotel. This was less than appealing. The idea of venturing out of a warm cottage not welcome.

Many guests at the cottage look curiously at my mantelpiece. Above the fireplace already stocked with *lakdi* for the winter there resides a ship in a bottle dated 1812 from a German ship. Recognised, if not by name, but by the flag of the Imperial German Navy. This four-masted sloop, intricately carved, with an unknown foreign hillside and town in the background, conveys both the boredom and dedication of seamen wasting their days while practicing this art. The inside of the bottle, probably a precursor to Old Monk, was constructed on the high seas in heavy weather. The ship in the bottle was carefully created and inserted. Then the masts erected by string and removed. The hole to be sealed forever by a plug. So, to the root of the story. When very young, on school holidays, I would work as a gardener's assistant for a Mrs Jacob. She owned Jacob's biscuits, still indispensable for cheese, and occasionally gave me tea in the garden. And paid me two shillings a day. When I left for London, Mrs Jacob took me to her study and said, 'Choose anything you would like.' There was a Cezanne and a Rembrandt on the walls. And lots of old furniture. I modestly asked for the ship in the bottle and got a currant bun to eat when cycling home.

The humidity of the valley can be oppressive. The monkeys cavorting on the balconies don't think so. Chipmunks still scamper. The flutterbies close their wings. The birds have gone home to roost, or brood. The trees are still. Not a branch of even a leaf whispers. Freddie is silent, looking soulfully as Labradors do. Is it thunder that I hear from the Himalayas or the passing of a tempo? A newly installed plant by the fireplace has wilted. Time for 'Third World War'. And a gin and tonic. Not, please Humphrey Hawksley, a war, in Doon. But you are welcome to join me for a gin.

I was alone in Delhi for a night, but early in the morning the resident night nurse bustles in. Obviously keen to advertise her attributes, to take my BP. After several attempts with her stethoscope, she diagnosed that I was 182/130. And fled. This was life threatening. I took this whole performance as an added bonus from a visit to Delhi. So I sunk into silent slumber only to be awakened by the family in-laws solicitously asking about my health. This was, they said, the end of the road. A small nephew bewailed the cost of sandalwood. As in so many Indian families, there is a confabulation over the bedridden by the bedside with doctors conferring. But I wanted to get back to Doon. Very soon. For a dinner given by Honey and husband General Shamsher Singh. A brother-in-law warned me, darkly, that if I should board the overnight train, I might never wake up. To flag off on the Mussoorie Express when it passes through Haridwar thereby saving everybody lots of loot. A doctor was summoned. My BP was 140/90. Very healthy he added, but drink less (note the less). No medicines, something of a first in India, but eat food. Doctors have been known to prescribe to their patients the entire contents of their chemist's shop. Over a period of time. If I had rupees one hundred for every time the doctors prescribe medicine. I would be a rich man. Or a doctor. But not a nurse.

At a children's school in Doon, it is often difficult to persuade the children to do things that they instantly hate. Like cleaning their teeth. So girls and boys sing:

> I am a pink toothbrush
> You are a blue toothbrush
> Won't you marry me in a haste?
> It would really be an awful shame
> To waste the same toothpaste.

A curious white cloud has descended. Freddie is hiding cowardly under the sofa. Martial law has set in, in the form of Kalyani with music playing in the background to keep up our spirits while thwarting the dog's. Freddie with a synthetic encrusted bone, certified safe by the vet to chew, drool on and discard.

I like Johnny Cash, but military music is more invigorating and more reminiscent of the British Empire which no longer exists. Country Western can become soporific. Best listened to in bed. On military music, a last overseas outing of the Royal Yacht (Britannia) to Mumbai, now sold by British politicians and the defence ministry as 'uneconomical.' It was instrumental in signing up orders for the UK of some two billion pounds. Shereen Mistry, my assistant, watched this proud old ship sail into the Bombay harbour, us having lunch in the Apollo bar on the top floor of the old Taj. Shereen having artfully persuaded the captain and Lord Chamberlain to arrange an unheard of tour of *Britannia* for journals while in the evening we watched, 'beating the retreat' by the royal marines on the Bombay docks. A fitting end to *Britannia* and to the Empire. The Indian GOC's wife sadly sobbed onto my tie. No matter, MCC ties, like their members, are supposed to last forever.

25

By Order of the British Empire, God Calls Me God

Mr George Fernandes came to town for the opening of 'Virasat', Uttaranchal's International Folk Live Festival at Dehra Doon. With a varied ten-day series of events beginning at the Dr Ambedkar Stadium in ONGC. Owing to a previous engage-ment, we were told, the Chief Minister did not turn up, but there will be international performances from Turkmenistan, national performances by Ustad Ahmed Mohammed Hussain of gazal fame, a play by Naseerudin Shah, a fold troop from Madhya Pradesh and a play, 'Maulana' by Tom Alter. Jaya Jaitely and Hanuman Dutta from Indonesia add to the international flavour. The down side is the traffic jams that these functions cause added to demonstrations at the

Mussoorie-Dehra Doon development authority over their apparent indiscriminate acquisition of land and the Students Union who very well demonstrated at the top of their lungs, their desire for a university while holding hands and blocking Rajpur road. There must be better ways to bring ones demands to the sympathetic eye of the public.

It was Lillian Skinner Singh's eightieth birthday. Actually, it was a week earlier, but the Mussoorie road was down with landslides so lunch was postponed and reinstated after the road was repaired. Kalyani cooked, aided by Jeeves. Old friends from the British High Commission in Delhi turned up at the cottage. My new chap and Jeeves cooked fried *baingan* to a turn; the kids frolicked, with Freddie watching them keenly. There are no dogs allowed in the British High Commission compound. What a waste of a child's education not to grow up with dogs. Later, Lilian's chocolate birthday cake arrived emblazoned by Sunday. 'For she's a jolly good fellow.' And we sang 'and so say all of us.' And meant it.

A very welcome letter from Rob Young thanking me for dinner in Doon, and to Sunday, and bidding us to his and Catherine's farewell in Delhi. Then back to Doon for a visit by Karan Thapar at the Dosco annual do-it-up. Who will they invite as chief guest this year? Amitabh Bachchan has already been done and so has the President of India. Could we hope for Preity Zinta?

I noted from Rob Young's letter that, he has now been appointed GCMG. There is, of course a pecking order in the British Honours system. The British Empire Medal given to junior staff engaged mainly in security matters is known as the 'Bloody Endurance Medal', then the Member of the British Empire is called 'My Bloody Efforts.' Then the high up Order of the British Empire is called 'Other Bloody Efforts.' Then to the Order of St Michael's and St George; CMG, 'Call Me God.' Knight Commander, KCMG, Keep Calling Me God.' But the peak of one's career is the GCMG, 'God Calls Me God.' I think the real gods, Hindu, Punjabi, Buddhist, Jain or Christian smile smugly on who is what.

The British High Commission cricket team arrived in Doon after a long absence to play against the IMA. This might have been fair from the devastating results of previous matches when the Gentlemen Cadets invariably triumphed and the officers commiserated over pink gins. This time it was different. The IMA Gentlemen Cadets were dismissed for a hundred, although Honey Shamsher Singh sitting next to me said that it was a hundred and one. The scorer, she declared was lazy. 'Send him up to Siachen.' In the event, in a limited overs match, the IMA won by two runs. It should have been three, grumbled Honey. As usual, the Shergills displayed a wonderful hospitality, which the high commission guests could not fault. A lunch and dinner. A valuable re-establishment of contacts formed years ago and inevitably through cricket.

I think, modestly, that my Hindi or Garhwali is slowly improving. No longer the tourist *shukriya*, but thank you and *dhanyawaad* get an appreciative nod. The roadside fruit sellers who used to palm off rotten plums now smile and dig out their good stuff. As the monsoon closes down, until the winter rain arrives, my household decided that Thursday is window cleaning day. Jeeves and the Delhi helper climb ladders to expunge the dirt and dust left after the summer. They do it with enthusiasm. Diwali rewards in the horizon of their minds! Jeeves' young son marches around proudly with a *squeegee*. Soon it will be time for the wood work and cane furniture to be licked with liniment. The walls of the cottage freshly white washed to appease the winter gods. Chestnuts from Mussoorie to be gathered to stuff in the Christmas turkey and the remainder roasted on an open fire. Holly from the hills, berries blooming. Mistletoe from Manali for a lucky kiss. Kalyani smiles, looking. Definitely Freddie. And a vintage Christmas pudding, courtesy Fortnum's and Masons. Sozzled in Old Monk with brandy butter after midnight mass on Christmas Eve.

A cacophony of sound bursts into the normally peaceful cottage garden in Rajpur. My neighbour's Rottweilers, not the most comfortable of cuddling companions begin with overture. Nayantara Sehgal's brood join for an andante. Freddie, snoozing, manages the slow movement. An invasion? Yes. A mountain multitude of monkeys are set on stripping my avocado tree. Then attacking the pubescent jackfruits. The dogs provided the crescendo, but dogs can't climb trees like monkeys do. They also do not like avocadoes. Jeeves and his little son throw stones and inevitably the monkeys throw them back. They are more accurate and reminiscent of the Australian fielding side. Monkeys retire, replete. Monkeys three, cottage staff zero. King monkey surveyed the scene with approbation. Freddie hides his head in shame. I have relief by laughing as one of the primates scampers away.

On the subject of kings. Lewis King dropped in to tell me that he had a hernia. He tried to stuff the protuberance back in, but to no avail. He was therefore en route to Disha Hospital to have his abdomen stitched up. Like me, he was apprehensive of a general anaesthetic but my Australian house guest, Dr John had told him that a local anaesthetic would suffice. I forgot to tell him that Dr John's idea of an anaesthetic was a large gin, adulterated only with ice and a slice of *nimbu* for decoration. Followed by a post prandial glass of Old Monk.

26

A Fishy Story

The day dawned with thunder and lightening in Rajpur. Most unseasonable, but it was of course the day of the Windlass Polo Cup final at the Indian Military Academy (IMA). Last year, the event was almost completely washed out by heavy rains. Was this to be a repeat? The gods relented and by the afternoon, the weather was fine, if muggy. The skydiving was remarkably accurate, the band display in perfect formation. The polo, which to me has always looked hazardous, was followed by a daredevil riding display. It was difficult to tell the difference between the two. Back to Oscar Wilde's description of fox hunting: the unspeakable in pursuit of the inedible. In the former case, a fox, and in the latter, a polo ball. In the evening Windlass and the IMA held a truly splendid dinner dance in the officer's mess. While the golden oldies munched and crunched, slurped and chirped, the youngsters were on the dance floor performing seemingly impossible maneuvers to mad music. At a relatively early time, the notable retired generals decided that it was time for bed. I could not but agree. The stars were up and shining bright. The moon was awake. The youngsters, unaware of the splendours of the sky, were more engaged in rapture and not nature.

The flood of visitors to Doon and especially to Mussoorie continues unabated. Should not the Northern Railways consider that regular residents might be awarded priority reservations? Or at least some honesty in ticket allocation? The foreign tourist allocation paid for in foreign exchange at New Delhi railway station booking office is a joke. The ONGC and the FRI have obtained unacknowledge and secretive block bookings. For themselves, families and friends. Which they often don't use. Take an example. A party of young lady Japanese tourists at New Delhi Station were heart-broken when their pre-confirmed tickets resulted in them being off-loaded just before the Shatabdi left for Haridwar. 'What do we do?' they cried. The station staff were stuffing wads of boodle into their wallets. I remonstrated and was told to mind my own business. The young Japanese will not return. Nor will their friends contemplate India as a destination of beauty and culture. They were left to the mercy of touts in a foreign environment. If India wants foreign tourists to visit, it must offer service and help with a smile. To return to the governor of Uttaranchal's adage, 'Lend a helping hand.'

A morning in Doon and I awoke to the sound of birds and to Miss Maali as she sweeps the steps. A perfect summer's day. Overnight the normally drab Jacaranda trees have suddenly burst into bloom, already scattering their tresses to form a delicate carpet of blue. So sudden to have arrived and so sudden to leave. Flame of the Forest brightly and brilliantly form a background to the deep green of the misty Himalayas. 'Where the blue of the night meets the gold of the day' with thanks to Bing Crosby. In the afternoon I win at bridge, playing against three redoubtable ladies of note. Twenty two rupees. Forget me, income tax wallaha, its for fun not for the loot! Then to light supper of iceberg lettuce begging to be doused in olive oil, cider vinegar consumed with Parma ham and juicy melon. 'Beatrix Potter's characters, the flopsy bunnies said that, 'the effect of eating too much lettuce is soporific'. So I slept.

Maali came in one morning proudly displaying some reading glasses which I had lost in the garden some days ago. He had found them in the pond while cleaning it. Sadly, in his excitement, three of my grown up goldfish had departed to wherever they go, to fish's nirvana. Out of the four adult goldfish, three were females. So I am left with hirsute male and five fledgling *bachas*. When quizzed on the manner of the ladies demise, Maali could only speculate that some large birds had eaten them. I rather doubt this speculation, but will monitor the garden closely for goldfish bones.

Most Embassies and High Commissions issue travel advisors when they consider it unwise for nationals of their country to visit a particular part of India. This is their duty, but not one which is often appreciated by the Central or State Government whose area and tourist trade is adversely affected. Luckily Uttaranchal, primarily a peaceful place has not been the subject of this adverse advice. Long may it remain so. There are many ways of reaching Doon and this is not a travelogue, but a guide based on some years of experience. Flying to Jolly Grant airport is expensive although it has a pretty good hospital next door. Then a long drive to Doon is not worth it unless one wants to show off. I balk at the bus. The national highway terrifies me as do the drivers. So that leaves the railways. 'If God meant us to fly' said Aunty Annie 'She would never have given us the railways'. To Doon by rail, there are three direct options all of which I have tried. My favourite remains the overnight Mussoorie Express which serves, but goes nowhere near Mussoorie and caters to travellers from that hill station. It is quite pleasantly comfortable providing you get a lower berth or as happened in the monsoon, a coupe to ones self. You meet interesting people on an overnight train. Not the Agatha Christie variety, not Hercule Poirot or Miss Marple. Then the

Shatabdi Express with first class deluxe chair cars and good food with service and a cockroach thrown in for free. Not cheap by Indian prices. The *naya* Shatabdi leaving Doon at the improbable time of five am is daunting. The return to Doon from New Delhi is at the more respectable time of three-thirty in the afternoon. My experience on this train was a travelling companion aged three obviously destined at an early age to enter the Guinness book of Records by screaming and shouting for six hours non-stop. And succeeded.

Politely escorting Sunday on her way out through the front door of the cottage, she declined. She must for her next visit, walk out through the kitchen. Tidying up? Checking for *keeras?* No. I always leave the house by the same door as arrive. New one! In London, in my youth, I left a girl friends home abruptly, having entered through the door and exited, on the arrival of her parents, through the window.

27

An Englishman at the Devil's Tea Party

Doon is ready for Christmas. Plastic toys and electric candles for ersatz trees. No legal felling of fledgling Christmas trees is allowed in Dehra Doon, although quite a lot takes place for those who want their living room floor littered with pine needles. And no mistletoe under which to enjoy a chaste kiss. I refuse to kiss or to be kissed under a plastic berry. No holly either. The cottage has two conifer trees which will serve as decorations. In my original home bordering the woods of Delamere, there are vast tracks of Christmas trees which the forest department would sell. But only on the condition that one paid for and personally planted five new ones. And round the tree, there would be presents. It is more rewarding to give rather than to receive.

My Christmas is spent in Delhi and the highlight for me is to leave a glitzy Christmas Eve party for the Midnight mass at the Rashtrapati Bhavan Church. It is always packed with an assortment of worshippers testifying to India's, hopefully to be continued, secular commitment. Then to the carols which are invariably interdenominational. *God rest ye merry gentlemen* is probably too chauvinistic. *Ding dong merrily on high,* the chorus from which is too demanding and reminiscent of the public hangings at Tyburn. So my favourite, sung in Latin, is, *Adeste fideles / Laeti triumphantes / Venite, venite in Bethlehem. Natum videte / Regem angelorum.* And the chorus, sung at first by the children in treble voice, the second by teenagers and the final glorious line by the congregation. *Venite adoramus in Bethlehem.* Tears flow aplenty. Hugs and kisses. Then home for an Old Monk and a mince pie.

Carol services in Doon are mainly interdenominational with a spectrum of participants from all religions. Having missed the carol service in Mussoorie, courtesy Ganga Ram hospital, but determined to join, wheelchair and all, the Presbyterian celebration at the urging of the Masseys. In a wheelchair and clad in a long back overcoat, one can conceal, tucked into one's leg bandage, a container of medicinal compound marked cough medicine. I was wheeled ceremoniously to the front, conveniently placed by an open door which had the advantage of affecting a speedy unobtrusive exit and the drawback of a fierce cold draught of wind on the back. The assembly was mainly South Indian, and a large number of Tibetans. The music was played professionally by an American lady with an electric organ (sic!), slightly bizarre as she joined in the men's solo. The girl soloist, pretty enough for ninety minutes immobilised in a chair, was delightful. Dakem Rongong sang like the proverbial lark and looked the part. Although I confess to never having seen or heard either. Jeeves tapped me on the shoulder and said that it was getting cold. So we departed, light in soul, but so graciously as a lark. I didn't stay for tea, but in the car turned and smiled down at Old Monk. I swear that he winked back. Clever chaps, monks. Most of the best and revered liquors come from monasteries.

I have always admired people with the ability to light fires. Real ones, with seasoned and dead wood. Not like in London where one has those fancy gadgets, fed by gas over plastinated coals. Quite convincing, but guests tend to chuck their cigarette butts into the pseudo fire which likes it not a bit. Nor does the hostess next morning, cleaning the grate in exasperation and touching up the plastic coals with the husband's boot polish. My late father was a wonderful lighter of fires. In those days the fire served to heat the water, and had attached a small oven for Sunday roast meat. Maali is a fire lighter par excellence. The wood is over a year old. Two solid logs comprise a military-style formation. On the top, wooden chips coat them like the icing on a Christmas cake with small hewn slivers. By the side is an antique wrought iron vessel filled with replenishments for the fire god. A bowl of water to add humidity. No need to poke and push. No room full of smoke. Maali retires contentedly, a job well done to puff a *beedi*.

Christmas would not be a festive season without a bit of devilry. I can't believe that Satan, sartorially suited by Saville Row (God can't afford their prices) and bedevilled by the stye in his eye as a result of another Irish virgin en route to the altar (Ingmar Bergman), has his Christmas delights. A young man, rejected by St Peter, name written ominously in red in this book of departed souls, was sent down to hell. 'You have three choices,' said the devil. The first is walking on coals of fire. The second, for the Irish was drips of Bushmills whiskey flavoured with *hari mirch*. The final option was a room filled with Englishmen, standing neck deep in a pool of shit, but drinking tea, eating chocolate biscuits and chatting heartily. 'This is for me,' the Englishman said. No sooner than he had entered the shit pool, sipped his tea, lunged for a biscuit when an Old Labour stalwart from the trade unions entered. 'Tea break is over,' she announced. Back on your heads. And don't forget to wash the cups.' On this note, Girl Sunday and I wish all our readers, M.J. Akbar and Joyeeta Basu and everyone in *The Asian Age* a very happy festive season and a successful 2004.

28

Thank God for India, Tolstoy Wrote Lolita

For me, Dussehra is synonymous with *singaras*. In Doon, we burn effigies of Ravana, Meghnad and Kumbhkarn, although not, I recommend, a suggested practice in Tamil Nadu where things are perceived differently. Here we deify Ram. Enjoy Ram Leela. I do. But don't forget the humble *singara*. Spawned in the cesspits and tanks of India, thriving on industrial waste these magic marvels with some form of osmosis emerge clean white, cool and crisp. Don't fry them, bake them, or cut them with a knife. Break their thick skins with your finger, then crunch and munch.

Do I want to live in Doon, I was asked. Die in Doon? Oh yes! In India no, but Doon is different. No school, hospital or public garden will bear my name. If it did, some stupid local government official would quickly change it to the name of a politician. Poor Keeling Road in Delhi. A modest lane named after one of my ancestors Sir Henry Keeling, who contributed to building the Rashtrapati Bhavan and Lutyens' New Delhi, is now Tolstoy Marg. What did Tolstoy do for India? I asked a politician. 'I have,' he said, 'read Lolita.' This was, of course, written by Vladmir Nabokov.

Once in India, I accompanied the Princess Royal on a visit to Ladakh. The aircraft of the Queen's flight, I was told, departed at seven-thirty am. Princess Anne would arrive at Palam at seven twenty-eight. The door of the aircraft would close at seven thirty am. Engines turning. She did and it did. I had taken along my superb secretary, Debra, and an equally excellent information assistant, Aditi Banerjee, the latter known as 'Po' or 'Problem Child' for her propensity for being charming to journalists and horrible to the British High Commission hierarchy. We breakfasted on bacon, eggs and Cumberland sausages served by white uniformed stewards. And landed at Leh on time. The Queen is known to become testy if schedules are not maintained. Prince Philip swears. He says that to be late for an engagement demeans the guests.

So to Doon Founders' Day. We were asked to be seated by one thirty. Girl Sunday and I were royally seated in the front row. Doscos were perched behind us having been in position by noon. We were all covered by a heat absorbing *shamiana*.

The rows of chairs on the dias were ominously empty. Promptly at ten past two we heard a helicopter arrive. But no guests of honour. They had, I later heard, gone for lunch at the Raj Bhavan with the governor, not with the governors of Doon School. The chief guest, doubtless brimming with goodwill for the one lakh school children he has promised to meet every year during his term in office, was apparently unaware that the eight hundred boys in the audience had not eaten lunch. Nor had the rest of us. The chief guest eventually arrived at three fifteen. Sunday was being chatted up by the class XII boys sitting behind us. Their comments on the very late arrival of the chief guest were scathing. Sunday pretended to look shocked, but smiled. She has been a school teacher. This new generation will, I feel adopt standards of behavior on which, in Doon, they were weaned and have embraced. Enough said, I put my *kalam* down.

Karan Thapar's critique in *The Hindustan Times* of Mr Kuldip Nayar's article about racism in Britain was timely. And accurate. In London, Karan and I live in approximately the same area, Notting Hill Gate and Holland Park. Karan's only problems of discrimination were, strangely, in Nigeria, where the information minister complained to me that the BBC had not sent a representative who was white. Neither my Indian wife nor Karan has had any racial discrimination in London. In Notting Hill, we have an annual carnival. The largest in

Europe, attracting two million visitors. The first day is for children. The second has floats which drive past with brightly dressed West Indians, Indian Indians, Pakistanis, Bengalis, Bangladeshis and the British. All singing loudly with a display of humour and racial harmony. So retreat Mr Nayar, to an ivory tower, and don your rose-tinted dark glasses. And represent your views somewhere else.

I was amused over newspaper articles reporting that Mr Jyoti Basu of Bengal was advising that the *dhoti* should be discarded. Presumably, for Saville Road or Raymond's. The most elegantly attired and one of India's most eloquent speakers will now be dressed as an Indian Englishman. In Doon, one can always identify an MLA. Dressed in a white starched crisp *kurta pyjama*, stretched to its pretentious political proportions, passing in his classy Cielo, horn hooting. The youth of Doon prefer Allen Solly and Adidas. So does Sunday.

29

To Have a House High on the Hill

It was time to reestablish my credentials and who better to begin with than Dehra Doon's District Magistrate, Ratna Raturi. Coincidentally and providentially her husband is DIG Police. I telephoned for an appointment and she said brightly, come now. So I did, with Sunday and we waited in her office for less than ten minutes. The lady Magistrate, a member of the IAS has had an interesting varied career in Andhra, Madhya and now is firmly seated in Uttaranchal. She was welcoming, frank and acknowledged that she was only forty years of age. A huge responsibility for somebody so young. Somehow as I have mentioned earlier, Civil Servants from which ever country seem to establish a rapport. We talked or rather, she talked about the difficulties of Dehra Doon, its increasing population and it being the defacto State Capital. The traffic is a serious problem. Various State Organisations are conjoining to work out a solution, but most have different solutions. The D.M. took this with the quiet amusement of a seasoned IAS officer. She had seen it all before and will doubtless see it again.

Then on to more serious business. Girl Sunday asked Mrs Raturi whether she had sensed any bias against her as a woman DM. The answer was a robust no. She frankly said that it was better being a woman because a man, the locals thought, could be more easily tempted to stray. Women of her rank were respected both as ladies and senior office bearers. Various supplicants arrived with masses of paper duly attested by some dubious court lawyer. One of the supplicants. Carrying a wooden stick was shamelessly begging for alms under the pretext of disability. The manner in which he waved his stick firmly on two healthy legs laid some doubt to his claims. One glance at him and Kalyani turned to me whispering he was a professional beggar, healthy enough to live off his fat. I could not but acquiesce. The DM having been stung by him in the past, gave a smooth smile relegating him to the back of the queue. She was happily talking to Kalyani and me about her job, her previous postings with the IAS and her commitment to her present assignment in Dehra Doon.

Our new governor, Mr Aggarwal, is adopting a higher profile than his predecessor. One innovative measure is to open the Raj Bhawan to visitors on a regular basis. Rather like the President of India opening the Rashtrapati Bhawan and its beautiful garden annually. Mr Aggarwal has organised a flower show and the committee (yes, another!) has asked me to write a piece for their complimentary brochure on herbs and spices which I shall happily do and look around seeking the treasures of the Raj Bhawan. Once in Srinagar, staying with B.K. Nehru and Forie Aunty, when he was governor, my young son was intrigued by a large embellished Kashmiri wooden box. He spent hours trying to find ways to get into it and to discover its treasures. After a week's failure and seeing his frustrated tears, Aunty Forie showed him the secret. Inside were her jewels, which she never wore, being still a plain and simple person. Then, as a punishment for his curiosity, he was, at the age of twelve, initiated into Kashmiri tribal dancing much to his horror. The young girls adorned him with necklaces of semi-precious stones. I took photographs and gave him the negatives for his next birthday. Whether he kept them or not, I do not know, but I suspect they were consigned to the fireplace. In those days, under B.K. Nehru's benevolent guidance, Kashmir was a simple, if underdeveloped, place. Let's hope and pray that it returns to that status.

In Doon, visitors will be pleased to know (I doubt) that property prices are on the rise. Some Sardarjis have been inspecting a few *bighas* next to me. They can probably afford it. Although the errant owners not having built a retaining wall and balcony have found that much of their property has slid into the cud. On the hill opposite, new piles of bricks have arrived and construction begun for yet another weekend cottage, visited rarely—possibly only when there is an 'r' in the month—but a good cocktail party feature in Delhi or Ludhiana. Back to the cud which falls away some eighty feet precipitously from my well-constructed retaining balcony. Through the cud in the monsoon, a small stream rushes into the valley below. It had eroded the silver oak trees which now lie prone, offering the delightful prospect of free winter wood. The cud is overgrown, but could be a place of delight. I hope, with the help of friends, to clean it up.

Dr S.S. Sandhu, vice-chairman of the Mussoorie – Dehra Doon development authority, recently met with some of the Doon Valley action groups, notably Clean Doon. Dr Sandhu had left the medical profession for a wider sphere of activities. His horizons were wider. After Noida, Chandigarh and Ludhiana, he set his sight on Uttaranchal having become a permanent member of the IAS cadre. He answered Clean Doon's comments with clarity. Sanitation is a priority and selected citizens in the neighbourhoods of Doon will have direct control over a number of sweepers with the authority to hire and fire according to the level of efficiency observed. As many of the citizens chosen to monitor will be retired military officers or school masters, let the sweepers beware. A disposal plant for plastic bags will be established. Hoardings which are ugly and ruin the countryside will be torn down as indeed one has been outside my cottage. Dr Sandhu explained that a large problem that the administration faces is the indifference of the public and the self-interest of the people whose illegal construction mean more money to them than does the environment in which they live. But, as Dr Sandhu remarked correctly, the state government and the people must conjoin in their efforts to preserve Uttaranchal as India's loveliest state.

The Clean Doon charity is a worthwhile, worthy organisation. But it has the freedom to express its views to the Uttaranchal senior civil servants who listen. At length, frequently interrupted by those who know better. A civil servant's life is not a happy one. Poor lads and lasses. Clean Doon is clear on its objectives. My gentle, humorous comment on the chairman's report, 'why should only dogs be sterilised?' did not find favour.

30

After Sunday, it Has to be Girl Monday

Girl Monday began work today, replacing Girl Sunday, who has decamped to Goa with the Cincinnati kid. In June, lunatic! Even the Germans and French know better. Goa in June is a sweat shop. Even the fishermen lie around, and snooze (more Coward in 'Mad dogs and Englishmen') and the fish are on holiday too. The hippies have already left by tortuous travel for Dharamshala to commune with the Buddhist monks. Monday and I met by happy chance in Dalanwala. Losing my way, I stopped at her house that was curiously numbered the same as the one for which I was looking, a *Times of India* journalist. Needless to say it was the wrong address but the owners knew the right one. The hospitable couple, (he with the State Bank of India) invited me in for a refreshing glass of water, while waiting for my hostess. Then their daughter arrived perched on a scooty. She had finished her Masters in Commerce and also a course in Mass Communication from Chandigarh and was looking for a job. So I offered her one. Sim and her parents came to the cottage for an interview, for which, I thought from Mrs Jain, that it was I who was being interviewed. Mother thought I was a good chap and Smriti now Sim is working for me and loves dogs. She has two and Freddy could smell future companions. So welcome, Girl Monday. We will test her out with Ruskin, Ashok Massey and Mr King at Dhanolti tomorrow.

Sim asked out of curiosity why I called my general factotum Jeeves. The reason I explained was simple, especially for anyone who is an aficionado of P.G. Woodhouse. Bertie Wooster's Jeeves would shimmer rather than walk. A regular willo-the-wisp, my Jeeves is the same. I can be sitting in a quiet and apparently deserted room, when magically a glass full of mother's ruin will appear at my elbow. Looking around for Jeeves, he has shimmered away to answer a ring at the front door of the cottage. Jeeves skimmed out and came back with an Airtel bill. Another bloody Monday (not Sim!). All I hear is the click of the kitchen door as Jeeves returns to the quarter. Also like the P.G. Woodhouse Jeeves, my clothes are laid out in the morning. Nor would I have the temerity to make my own choice. This would cause a frown and returning from my bath, I would find that his dress sense has prevailed.

Visitors to the cottage are always welcomed but the two new guests were specially so. Perching prettily, preening on my mountain pine. One yellow, not a golden aureole but as rare as the nightingale in Berkeley Square. The first, I learnt from my bird book was a Finn's baya, or yellow weaver. Normally in pairs, this bloke was desolate in solitude. Finn's bayas normally sing in chorus. This chap was silent but stayed. I gave him some boiled rice until Freddy, getting jealous, chased the weaver away. The second identified as a small green bee eater, Merops Orientals, was more persistent. Her thin curved beak pecked at the glass of the cottage windows until I satisfied her with peanuts. She left with a chirrup. Soon to return.

Lunch again, in Delhi with Moni Chaddha. It is so refreshing to meet regularly with a Former Foreign Secretary who is deprecating and not opinionated. After his ditty about growing older, which we are not except in terms of years, I penned one for him.

'Age is a time when your bones start to creak
When the stairs are making you weak
When the girl in the bus will offer up her seat
and sit, cross legged demurely showing her feet'

I bought for my in-laws in Delhi some Uttaranchal strawberries. It is too hot here for golf and tennis but the

Uttaranchal strawberries, like the Garhwali girls, thrive on th
heat. Remarkably succulent. A niece, who is studying Hote
Management in New Delhi, suggested an additive of ice-cream
Fine. But chocolate chip and strawberries! 'Why not add
peanut butter?' I suggested. She noted down my recipe for
culinary disaster, I dined out that evening.

31

If I Had Eighty Million Pounds, I Could Do with a Blue Lagoon or Two

Priests and politicians have much in common. They both revel in a captive audience and will use it endlessly. Luckily, I don't have to endure political speeches. I write about people and places not about politicians, whatever my feeling might be for the greater good of India. But I girded my loins for the Reverend Bishop of Agra at the hundred and sixty-eighth anniversary of Christ Church on the Mall in Mussoorie. A lovely old Church. The stained glass windows at St Paul's in Sisters Bazaar differ from those at Christ Church. These are a translucent yellow, while those in Christ Church are in vivid reds, blue and greens. Sim, looking delightfully sleepy in the morning, me feeling no better, arrived at the Mall where I was charged a hundred rupees to enter. Was there a discount for those worshipping God I asked and got an unsympathetic sneer but he asked whether I was the Bishop from Agra. 'Would that have got me a discount?' Perhaps, but not from God.

Sim and I arrived early for the Church service. I was in time for an early gin and tonic. It was a sensible precaution, for the service lasted for two hours. The congregation varied, after Indians, Tibetans and an assortment of nations from Wood Stock International School, who provided much of the music, which was brilliant. A largo from Handel, a Fugue for solo violin by Bach and Antonin Dvorak's *Allegro F. Major*. A *Pavitra Atma* sung by little school children. Finally '*All people that on earth do dwell*' by the congregation.

Lillian and the Skinner's were there. Although, I suspect that Lillian might have dozed during the sermon on which I return to the opening point. Unlike politicians the Right Reverend Cutting was fairly brief, only fifteen minutes. I declined Holy Communion first as I explained to Sim that they watered the wine. Secondly, I don't subscribe to hypocrisy. Each to his own beliefs. But for me watered wine on Sunday mornings is unacceptable, especially to an Irish man. After the service the Templeton's asked us for tea. I pleaded another engagement. Very nearly tempted but for the proximity did not repeat what my vicar in Hampstead said after morning church 'I have done my duty to the Lord. Now we must appease the publican'.

Sim and I did.

A very silly, sad and somber telephone call. Anonymous. Not from Doon but probably London instructing me not to write bad things about Mrs S. Gandhi. 'I don't write about politicians' I replied. A crude attempt at intimidation. Not necessarily by the Congress high command. So I will tell you a true story about the former Prime Minister. Some years ago I was in Patna, for the British High Commission following an election campaign, having drawn the short straw and got Bihar. To pay for my over rated and grossly priced hotel in Patna, I left obliged, despite the heat to seek interviews with the local parties, the Congress and the BJP. The local parties had no interest and had probably not heard of the British High Commission. The Congress failed to respond to my invitations, the BJP sent a young man around to invite me and my colleague, Aditi Banerjee, for breakfast the next morning. Aditi, known as Po said, 'Pull the other leg.' At six-thirty the next morning there was a knock at my door. The BJP man and Po were ready to pick me up. Po was in an aggressive mood but Mr Vajpayee responded courteously in perfect English, with a joke or two and was incredibly impressive. On the way back to the sweaty hotel I asked Po whether she found Mr Vajpayee attractive. There was a long silence. 'Perhaps'. So my best wishes to Shri Atal Bihari Vajpayee. Do not fade like Cheshire cats leaving only your smile. I shall read your poems when I read Hindi but remember your achievements.

Fame at last! Profiled by Anjali Nauriyal, in *The Times of India* with a photograph that unusually does not resemble the respected Jug Suraiya with a hangover. Girl Monday's father, returning from an official trip from Delhi, was thrilled that his daughter was hitting the headlines. It is good to make parents happy and proud. Sim gave me that lip-gloss look while tucking into mangoes and marshmallows. Doon and Ellora's best. Freddy was abashed. When do I get my picture in the newspaper? He growled. The matrimonial alliance paper of *HT*, I suggested. Woof Indian Kennel Club be warned.

I read that some ennobled N.R.I. (Mittal, I think) has spent eighty million pounds sterling for a house in Kensington Palace Gardens. Near the Indian High Commission residence. Garaging for fourteen cars. No space for Ambassador or Maruti models. I hope that the Royal Borough makes him pay a lofty property tax which will become his status. And might bring mine down a bit. The Indian High Commissioner living nearby with the Russians next door and Kenisington Palace are exempt from tax. If I had eighty million pounds I would spend ten or so on books. Various and variable. An original Marquise De Sade with illustrations held, it is said, in the Vatican sanctorum. Then an Island in the Seychelles; white sand, a coral reef and an old Beaver float plane to land on the lagoon. But not the Kensington Palace Gardens. So I leave Lord Mittal (Not Mithai I trust) with a ditty. Transmogrified from Noel Coward.

If I Had Eighty Million Pounds

'The stately homes of Kensington
How proudly do they stand
To show the working-classes
Who really rules the land!'

32

To be in Doon, Now that Monsoon is Here

Auspiciously, the monsoon in Doon has descended, pelting, not pitter-patter. Freddie, who is now addicted to Jacob's cream crackers, is learning how to open the *jaali* doors with his long Lab tongue. So far unsuccessfully. Girl Monday has become quite attached to a daily dose of Pimms with extra *nimbu*, cucumber rind and Sprite. Sliced pears, mangoes and apples are a bigger obligatory. For those anxious parents with children drinking alcohol and doing drugs, I told Sim's mother, Mrs Jain, that Pimms is innocuous and the fruit content benefits the skin, although Sprite is not so good for the waistline. Mrs Jain was convinced, almost.

Back to the monsoon. I had planned to drive on Sunday to Dhanaulti, Sister's Bazaar and then to Cloud's End to Christ Church for Sunday service. Then maybe navigate the precarious steps to the Snake Temple. The gods of the Himalayas decided otherwise. Thunder, lightning and incessant rain. Ruskin Bond advised against the trip. The roads were blocked with rocks and with poor rich Punjabis escaping to the safety of Amritsar. So peace at the cottage. No *bijli* of course, no diesel. Another bloody strike. No TV servers, although the Asian Cup cricket final came on time for a dramatic if predictable win by Sri Lanka. The gods of the Himalayas rumbled either in appreciation of Lanka's performance or displeasure of India's dismal showing. Then despatched the monsoon clouds. Next day was Monday and as Girl Monday reminded me, a working day.

As the train tumbles down in Doon, I read Alec Guinness's book *My Name Escapes Me*. In his long career as an actor he played so many parts that the title of the book was appropriate. Seven separate roles in *Kind Hearts and Coronets*, then transformed into an evil looking robber in *The Lady Killers*. For me he was the quintessential actor. I met him once outside Fortnum and Mason's in Piccadilly. It was raining and we both were wearing hats. I recognised him immediately and doffed my *topi*, he raised his, gave me a droll smile and passed by.

There have been many amusing incidents in the British House of Lords. There is this famous story of Churchill, in the

House of Commons, who was questioned by an aggrieved Lady Asquith, during World War II. When Churchill, in deference to protocol, left his cigar and brandy in the lobby, Lady Asquinth said, 'If I were your wife, I would poison your brandy.' To which Churchill replied drolly, 'Madam, if I was unfortunate enough to be your husband, I would drink it.'

Our new Director General of Police, a lady, is pleasant, personable and a dedicated officer. There was a murder of a widow on Rajpur Road, following which Nayantara Sehgal was burgled, thankfully, with no harm to herself. The thieves took out an almirah containing valuable historical papers written by her mother. The robbers having forced open the almirah obviously had no idea of the treasures inside which were almost dumped in a ditch. DGP Kanchan Bhattacharya let no grass grow under her feet. Extra police were stationed outside Nayantara's house. She then, with full police cooperation, organised a meeting with local residents which the police attended, headed by the DGP, who along with other officers for nearly two hours, courteously and with humour, answered questions, Her basic message with which I agree, is to know your neighbour, know your local police better and live as a community with regular meetings to attend to each other's fears. Full marks to the Uttaranchal DGP and her policing policy.

On the Mussoorie Express I had, two years ago, met Mr R.P.S. Katwal, Director General of the Indian Council of

Forest Research and Education at the FRI in Doon. I eventually phoned up a bit late but Mr Katwal was accommodating. He was leaving for Delhi the next day and suggested Dr Paramjit Singh who then showed us around. My specialised subject that day in the height of the monsoon in August, was water conservation. It transpired that the ICFRE were mainly analysing which tree and shrubs store water in their natural catchment areas rather than manmade tanks, but as usual on such visits, one discovered a separate vein of gold. Sim saw some wastepaper baskets apparently made of bamboo. With the FRI's overall commitment to the preservation of existing trees, the ICFRE has found a solution. This is the *lantana*, a weed in bush form, with pink flowers often seen on the roadside. It was, I remembered, introduced by the New Zealanders to prevent erosion. This it achieved. But it grew and spread like the triffids. It is deep-rooted and thought completely useless as the leaves are inedible to cattle. But the FRI discovered its uses. The shrub they cut and convert to wood which is cured, is being manufactured as a cottage industry by villagers in Uttaranchal and Haryana. If machine-pressed heavily, it forms basic material for making side stools and other useful articles. The advantages being that the weed, known to the villages as *besharam*, now provides a valuable alternative to cutting trees. So another gold Toothpick award to the Forest Research Institute. Another bonus is a source of income to poor villagers whom the ICFRE is encouraging to set up workers' cooperatives. So you might one day furnish your fashionable drawing room with weed, or *besharam*.

A newly acquired doctor in Doon remarked kindly that I looked well more than my years. Sim agreed. But you are as old as you look and feel. So I leave you with a little poem.

When Freddie and I go down to the shops
For milk and cheese
And bread and chops
We look at all the wrinklies
There,
Who shuffle around the
Shelves and stare.
And tell ourselves when we
Are old,
Our hands won't shake, we won't lose hold
And when we are half way home we'll find
We've left our cheese and
Chops behind.

33

An Independence Samosa for Freddie

Girl Monday remarked to me, in some wonderment that the Doon Valley has so many unexplored treasures. I knew that and said rather pompously that it was good for her to find out for herself. We had returned from another visit to the Forest Research Institute where the indefatigable and enthusiastic Dr Paramjit Singh is helping Sim prepare a series of articles on the institute's diverse research programme. He is also arranging field trips to villages who are benefiting from the results. There is gold to be found, with little mining in the Garhwal and Shivalik hills. But for one with a 'Mirch Masala' mind, there is a froth of gossip to which, now that I am accepted by most, I am privy. Dehra is like a long running BBC programme 'The Archers and Everyday Story of Country Folk', which scrapes the veneer from their genteel lives to reveal the dark secrets below. Like in the Falkland Islands where isolated settlements could communicate with Stanley only by radio. Naturally everyone listened in. Especially to calls for the doctor. So the news of unmarried Betty's bun in the oven, or Charlie's case of the clap was soon common currency. But not uncommon as currencies.

Independence Day in India is not such a great event or celebrated in the manner in which the Republic Day is celebrated with some foreign dignitary with the President on parade at Rashtrapati Bhavan. The Rajasthani camels and the elephants along with the delightful dancers from the North-East swirl and twirl in their National Dress. This is secular India. But the Independence Day at the Governor Agarwal residence was also quite fun. Sim and I reached one hour earlier to avoid the traffic and were greeted by Aloka, the Governors public relation officer, working with him for his project on higher study scholarships. Raj Bhavan was decked for the occasion with tea and samosas, all served impeccably by white-suited waiters. The great and the good of Uttaranchal were present and Sim and I were made welcome. I was not allowed to take Freddy. Nor parents their children. But I took Freddy home a vegetarian samosa, which he appreciated possibly more than the Governor.

34

Plain Tales from the Foothills

Christmas is coming. The turkey, resigned to its fate, is getting fat. The Bharat Sanchar Nigam delivered their 2004 directory along with their latest bill. A double edged Christmas present. Their directory, like my bill contains lots of surprises, a sort of Christmas stocking. Their 'deliverywala' arrived wet. We had early winter rains in Dehra and snow in the Himalayas. Then to the directory, there is much to research for months and interviews galore, The Anthropological Survey of India, the Botanical Survey, the Central Silk Board (Forest Grown Silks), the Indian Institute of Remote Sensing, the Defence Standardisation Cell and the Bee Keeping Centre. I decided on the last. Like Pooh the bear, I like home produced honey. The BSNL telephone operator, whose voice sounds like a prune sucking lemon with salt in vinegar, told me that bees do not exist. Tell that to the Queen Bee. Drones, the queen consorts are on their way to the telephone exchange.

As Christmas is arriving, Christ Church Mussoorie held its annual service with nine lessons and carols. The cathedral was cold as a crypt. The service was varied. Children from the Hindustan Church sang beautifully in Hindi songs like *Pavitra Atma*, *Sare Shristi ke Malik tumhi ho* and many others. These were interspersed with English hymns like 'O Come, O Come Emmanuel', 'While shepherds watched', sadly not in Latin, 'Adesti Fideles' as taught to me in school. There was no sermon, thank the Lord. After a brief cup of tea I repaired with the Skinner sisters and Col Mahendroo to Sikander Hall for the obligatory gin and tonic, when we congratulated Sylvia on her reading of one of the lessons. Before the Church Service I met Virgil D. Meidema, Regional Director Asia Subcontinent with the American Soyabean Association. He is interested in restoring the William Hill Organ at Christ Church which was installed in 1880 but has not functioned since the early 1960's. It stands or rather sits as a beautiful but unused monument. A British company is prepared, at a price of thirty lakh, to put it into working order. It would be used for services of worship as well as for practice by music teachers and students. Once again the sound of the organ will resonate through the hills of Doon to the glory of the Gods.

Slim Sim and I called on the newly appointed Lt General K.K. Khanna who has taken over recently from Lt Gen Negi at the Indian Military Academy. He has had a varied career and was wounded in operations during his tenure in Jammu and Kashmir. He is from the Infantry Division of the 16th Jat regiment. A few days later there was a Passing out Parade by gentlemen cadets with Lt Gen Vij, Chief of Army staff, being the guest of honour and presenting prizes to the leading GC's. The colours of the IMA were ceremoniously brought on to the Parade Ground and everyone stood. Luckily Jeeves had parked the Qualis in the diplomatic parking area next to the cars from the Malaysian High Commission, there to celebrate the Passing Out of the Prince of Johar. A driver helped me over the fence with my rickety knee. The cadets, now officers, were throwing their caps and turbans in the air in joy.

Doon in December is a time for festivities and celebrations. Girl Monday took off Sunday to take me to the Himalayan Torch Bearer Christmas function. I am still in the dark about what Torch Bearers do. Ashok Massey told me that they are an Australian funded college of Evangelists and with Pentecostals who eschew all visible signs of the Cross. I found out that they do not believe in idols or gowns but only in God. A little similar, I am told, to Jesus Witnesses who used to bang on my door in Notting Hill in London telling me not to use doctors. The Lord would provide. I believe in the Lord in many variants. But the Gods are impunable. Doctors are more reliable.

Things in Doon are hotting up. Promila Kaul of the Association of British Scholars and the Uttaranchal Health System Development project me for a seminar for The Prevention and Management of Heart Attacks and related problems. Their advice was predictable. Besides being hereditary, smoking is of course fatal as is being over weight. Hypertension is a disaster. I spoke to Dr Samir Swami from Boston who demonstrated that banging five fingers of the right hand against your chest might prove effective. He also said that Indians are more prone than others to Heart Disease. He prescribed a regular diet of asprin and disprin and long walks.

35

Why Gin Always Acts Like a Tonic

You tend to meet odd people on the Indian Railways, I don't mean only the ticket collectors. I sometimes get lucky. A pretty girl, who cried all the way to Haridwar. Not ready to be consoled with a gin and Schweppes. A failed arranged marriage. Not having provided a dowry. Could I help? No way at my age.

My next guest was one Dr Mishra who was taking his daughter to join the Jolly Grant Hospital as a medical student. I am never quite sure what neuro-surgeons do, although he remarked that a twist in my wrist could welcome his surgical attention. I thought gin and tonic would be more beneficial, whereupon the good doctor sighed and went to sleep having given up on enticing me to his clinic in Agra. I had a gin and tonic and did the same.

In Delhi my favourite hotel is the renovated Imperial with their long avenue of trees. Their lithographs, although not original, are tastefully framed. The Emily Eden suite especially. Emily was a remarkably adventurous lady travelling on her own through a male dominated North India and abruptly dropping in for a meal with the Mughals. They treated her with courtesy, although with some amazement. Emily had a fine hand in using original vegetable dye colours. She created portraits which are still as vivid as they were two hundred years ago. In London, Annette Strover as in her diminutive flat in Chelsea has a rare collection, but she, like me, favours Ganeshji. For Hindus, Ganeshji is considered to be very auspicious, the God of luck and happiness. Any kind of new beginning is done in his name. The fireplace in the cottage is flanked with an old stone Ganeshji on one side on whose feet I reverently keep fresh blossoms. On the left there is another Ganeshji, smaller, in soapstone, and in front of him is a silver elephant bell. Soapstoneji is a newer acquisition than the venerable fat bellied Ganesh, which has been with me for over thirty years. In London there were some spurious stories about God drinking milk. I tried it on Ganeshji. Failure. Meanwhile, Annette in her 80s in London with a wonderful collection of Ganesh, still visits Nepal annually and energetically plays elephant polo.

Sim was patiently waiting for me to collect her in Doon. We went to work with what she now calls the 'Lappy' which was supposed to be housed in a new coat from Cottage Industries with a solid shoulder strap. Although she decided it was not sufficiently impressive, she took it anyway. Sim tries to write poetry. I advised that Keats is romantic, but Milton is boring. It's much more fun to write something humorous. Give me an example she said, so I thought of a poem.

Really Sim you are not so slim
Take time off work to go to the gym
Exercise before and always after dinner
Only then will you get slimmer.
Your parents will be proud

The Bobby Cash concert hosted courtesy of **Kanti Bajpai** in the Rose Bowl, Doon School in aid of the Leprosy Mission was hugely successful. Ruskin Bond was the guest of honour and was staying at the cottage. He confided in me that he hated giving speeches. Later, dinner in the Master's Dining Hall— hosted by Harihar Lal, the deputy headmaster whose father wrote some of the most renowned books about the Doon Valley —was a pleasant if sober end to the evening. Girl Monday winked at me sipping cold Coke and ate Dosco fare. She had earlier slipped away from the concert to ensure that Jeeves had eaten. Escorted through the extensive Doon School grounds by a senior boy whose name was Ali. Jeeves had eaten.

Nevertheless. I breathed a sigh of relief at Sim's return to the Rose Bowl. Mr Harihar Lal smiled and said I told you so.

The next day we were giving lunch for Ruskin Bond who was also my houseguest and Bobby Cash and family were invited. Our guest list totalled about thirty-five and we had just enough plates, although Sim's mother had sent an extra dozen. Food was arranged in plenty by Sim and Jeeves. Chicken, mutton curry, *dal makhni*, *matar paneer*, *allu dum*, *bharvan bhindi*, rice and *roti* followed by fruit and ice-cream. Mr Bond sat like Buddha enjoying a gin and tonic. Lt Gen (Retd) Mau Shergill and Rindi, the now chairman of the Punjab Public Service Commission, had come from Patiala. His successor, commandant at the Indian Military Academy, Lt Gen Negi and his wife, the latter recovered from a perilous hang-gliding experience were joined by retired Lt Gen Shamsher Singh and his family. He, having read his invitation, had procured and looked fetching in a droopy hat. Lewis King ambled in fresh from Dhanaulti. Sanjeev Chopra, secretary, Uttaranchal Industries came with an invitation for the launch of his book, *Ten Thousand Crores: A personal Memoir of Uttaranchal's Industrialisation*, the following day at Raj Bhawan. Ashok Massey and his wife Aparna came along with the eminent Dr Vijay Kumar, renowned for his expertise in reconstructive surgery on leprosy patients. Also Anjali Nautiyal, *Times of India* correspondent in Doon. And a host of others.

Although Ruskin Bond was the *eminence grise* of the occasion, busy autographing books for children and adults, it was Bobby Cash who stole the show. It is one thing to see someone on stage giving a lively performance before an invited audience. It is a completely different experience to have Bobby sitting at the end of the sofa in the cottage, playing and singing his western country music, responding generously to requests for old favourites. I think we had *Blue Suede Shoes*. One of my favourites. He is too young to play *Lady in red*. This was no pantomime performance. Whatever Bobby does, it is for real. His commitment to charities in Doon Valley including the Leprosy Mission must conflict with his career as 'The Indian Cowboy' in Australia and also his recording sessions and documentary film. He magically juggles both to great effect. His international debut album *Cowboy at Heart* is a success in Australia and so will it be in India. Uttaranchal should be proud of their star. He and Ruskin were guests who made me feel privileged.

36

Why Notting Hill Could have been Pretty Putney

Prior to leaving for London via Delhi on the Mussoorie Express, slim Sim took me for a pre-pay and early Birthday lunch diffusing all my devious devices to pay the bill. Much to the awe of the maître d' and the waiters. The Kitty ladies at adjacent tables playing house deafened our conversation. I couldn't eat all of the butter chicken and Manchurian so Sim took it home for her dogs. In the afternoon, with the pre-monsoon rain pitter-pattering with Tchaikovsky's 1812 in the background, we wrote bits and bobs. 'I'll be very bored while you are away' said Girl Monday. She looked as mournful as my golden Lab, Freddy. Freddy will get some upper-class dog biscuits from 'Fortnum' in London and slim Sim the latest Oxford Dictionary from 'Hatchards' next door.

It has, over the years, been a tradition to spend birthdays in London. This July was no exception for lunch at my club 'The Oriental' situated off Oxford Street; I celebrated with a carafe of the club claret. Then to liver and onions with mashed potatoes which is a curiously English delicacy. Rarely, if ever, seen in India, except at Chandresh Kumari's Home in Himachal. She, a former Rajya Sabha M.P., now a State Minister. Chandresh of the Udaipur Royal family and husband Aditya a Himachal Maharaja own a guest house below Mclowdgunj where I stayed free as a family member. In the mornings Chandresh and I would drive to her liverwallah, then to drink beer on their lawn with Aditya while Chandresh divided her time between cooking and constituents. A wonderful couple. As they say in Ireland 'Not a bad bone in their bodies'.

Back to the birthday. An old friend in London, Bernard, photographer to the Queen gave me lunch. Cooked in his Notting Hill house by him and his companion Pearly, a Philippine lady. Despite knowing that I dislike late and heavy meals, lunch was served at seven in the evening. Homemade fishcakes, cooked in Virgin olive oil, with a miscellany of salads. Raspberries and cream to follow. I abstemiously sipped a single gin and tonic while discussing England's dismal summer in cricket, football and tennis. 'I blame it on Blair' said Bernard. I could not but agree. Iraq was his mistake. Compounded by the failure to condole with the family of a British soldier, executed by Saddam's supporters.

Sim told me sternly on the telephone that I was not in London to dilly dally, drink claret and eat Scottish roast beef. 'Write and send your copy on time' she said, which I did. In London where I live for a month of the year there are some delightful parts of Notting Hill now famous after Hugh Grant and Julia Robert's film which had nothing to do with my London homeland. It could have been entitled Ealing Common or Pretty Putney. But the film sent our house prices soaring. And on the downside crime and therefore insurance costs escalated. But I love Notting Hill Gate although not quite as much as Dehra Doon in India. Our private garden square, second only in size to Buckingham Palace accessed only by a key. The lovely local pub, where barmaids will chat for hours for free, never accepting a drink. And they are consumed with curiosity about India, Garhwal and the Himalayas. 'Is it safe?' they ask. 'Safe as houses', I reply, apart from the occasional earthquake and me.

Gold Toothpick of the month goes to the Indian High Commission in London. Pawan Verma the new head of India's very successful Nehru Centre in London. An old friend from his days in the Eternal Publicity Department of the Ministry of

External Affairs and his charming wife came to dinner. Pawan used to work in the Ministry with Aftab Seth who recently retired as Ambassador in Tokyo. Aftab was the best man at my wedding and probably saved my life. On the day before the nuptials we had a raucous stag party culminating in my being bitten by a potentially rabid dog. Aftab insisted that I should immediately consult a doctor who prescribed a course of anti-rabies injection which in those days were administered one each day for the next fourteen days in the stomach. There was strictly no alcohol allowed. So for me it was a dry 'shaadi'. After seven times around the fire with the pundit intoning for all his worth, Dr Charat Ram said 'Enough is enough, the marriage is made and if you go on longer you won't get paid'.

I miss Freddie the dog, the wild mountains but not the even wilder parties in London which continue until the early hours of the morning when I hope to be fast asleep and dreaming. When I return to Doon this month, it will be Freddie's first birthday. A romp through the woods chasing tigers. A doggie veggie pie or a cream cake? He should be so lucky. Soon in Doon, after the Monsoon to enjoy crunchy *singaras*.

Meanwhile, in London, the July rains have begun in concert with the Monsoon in Doon, ready to wash out the cricket and the rest of us. Unlike London rains, when the Monsoon arrives in the Himalayas there is no gentle pitter-patter but the Gods send down their full fury to lash us and welcome me back while we all look to the roof to see if we have a leak. The electricity is of course permanently down and so are the telephone lines to Delhi. Sim is still bored in my absence which I took as a compliment, so I penned a poem to cheer her up.

'Young Sim you are not so thin
But no one can ever call you fat
And Sim when you make a joke or smile
Done with all honesty and without guile
In Dehra they appreciate your form
In India, that's the norm
So that's that!'

37

Why I'd Never Confess to Monks, Young or Old

Delhi was seriously hot for April. My hacking jacket, impeccably styled, but bought on the cheap from Marks & Spencer's clung to me like a wet suit, but without the oxygen cylinders. The Shatabdi as usual, on time. Food and service excellent. A blind eye from the stewards, who by now know my habits well, my cough mixture aperitif. Behind me a cleric of the Catholic faith but with Irish origins had also a tickle in his throat, or so he said. So, we discussed transubstantiation and the use, by good Catholic girls, of contraceptive pills. He joined me in Old Monk with a chorus by us both from Lily the Pink who invented the medicinal compound. Much to the surprise of the other passengers on the train as it roared through Raipur (no stop) to Meerut where only two minutes were allowed, so announced the dulcet tones of a female voice on the intercom. So you better disembark quickly. Not that there were many takers for Meerut. But where oh where, Northern Railways, are those delightful female stewards of yesteryear? They could enliven the journey with a smile and a laugh. 'Do you,' the Irish father asked 'wish for me to hear your confession?' I thought, on balance, not.

The Dehra Doon and Uttaranchal civil servants both live up to the description. Nita Roy's son is a Bollywood boy, a personable, film producer who wants to film, with assorted hordes, the Kumbh Mela. But he needed permission. The chief secretary and the tourism secretary were both available to talk on the phone and were helpful as always. Mr N.N. Prasad, tourism secretary went out of his way to facilitate the necessary permits. I asked Mr Das, home secretary, whether he would go to the *mela*. 'If I do,' he replied, 'I shall be in the security of a surveillance structure'. I asked Mr Prasad the same question. No, he replied. Neither shall I. I shall stay in the quietude of the cottage and watch the film on television. While applying for a licence to open a liquor shop and make some money.

The second Toothpick award of the month goes to Zee TV. On a day when the fifth one-day cricket match was eagerly watched, with test matches to follow, they chose to screen a revolting movie depicting the atrocities which took place after

Partition. We all know it happened. But, at a time in the history of blossoming India-Pakistan relations, two nations cementing their relationship on the sacred ground of a cricket pitch in Lahore, how could they feature a film which derided both countries? Many leading newspapers have descried Hindus living in Pakistan, and India is home to the second largest Muslim population in the world. Perhaps the owners of Zee had gone for a long lunch. Certainly not appreciating the mood of India and Pakistan.

38

God Proposes but BSNL Disposes

Uttaranchal has celebrated the States fourth birthday. Sim and I were invited to Raj Bhavan for evening tea and recital by the Air Force band. We arrived to find a pall of flames and smoke lighting up the gardens. 'Was this an early Diwali party?' I asked. Regretfully not. The huge *pandal* erected in the Governors garden had caught fire and was burning merrily just half an hour before the programme started. Everything was reduced to ashes. Except for the Air Force band, who extracted themselves with the speed, if not the accuracy, of a MIG-23. Sometime later the loyal Fire Brigade arrived and laid out hose pipes which although quelling the flames, increased the thick black smoke rising to the clear blue skies. I sat comfortably on the veranda of Raj Bhavan and watched the spectacle. It was an electrical fault, so said the ADC. I gently and respectfully reminded him, and the governor of Guy Fawkes and the Gun powder plot.

'In Britain to err is human but to really mess things up you hire an electrician'. The Air Force band hastily reassembled and did their best. They had specially flown in from Pune and the Air Force Red Devils demonstrated their skills of para-jumping and freefall in the morning. It takes quite a lot to jump from an Indian Air Force aircraft from a height of a thousand metres. The evening was complete in the dusk with late tea and delicious plum cake. We said goodnight to the Governor and then congratulated the Chief Minister ND Tiwari on the occasion.

In Delhi for my mother-in-law Sumitra Charat Ram's ninetieth birthday. It was a gruelling day for her. If I ever reach ninety ears of age, which the Delhi doc reckon I might, nice optimistic chap, my day would be spent looking longingly at the Himalayas, absorbing gin and tonic. Sumitra has led an interesting life. She married Charat Ram soon to be Dr Charat Ram against her parents wishes. It was an enduring love match. The strict father-in-law the late Sri Ram sent them by sea to England to attend the coronation of Queen Elizabeth II, attended by Sumitra's brother, the late, Dharam Vira ji. They returned by sea laden with goodies to be stocked in *almiras* for dispensation at family weddings. Sumitra soon developed a love for Indian music, dance and drama. And with help from her friends and business colleagues she established Bhartiya Kala Kendra. The Bhartiya Kala Kendra both on the National and increasingly on the International level has been promoting Indian culture. Bharatnatyam, Oddisi, Kathak and Manipuri dances are now taught to Indian as well as foreign students.

One of the promoters of Sumitra's institution was Pundit Ravi Shankar, whom I sat next to at the evening festivities. He had very kindly agreed to play music at my engagement party thirty years ago. I was sitting next to my father-in-law to be, who whispered in my ear 'Do you like Indian Music?' 'Not much' I said. We both went to his room where he lit a cigar, more for effect than pleasure, offered me a scotch and took one himself which he looked at but barely sipped. I had two large ones and cruised to my flat in Malcha Marg when Pundit Ravi Shanker was reaching his zenith.

Toothpick award of this month is donated in spades to BSNL and VSNL, our telephone service providers, who are dedicated to serve but don't. I tried calling my home telephone number through mobile from Delhi, only to be informed my telephone number 'Does not exist'. On returning to Doon I telephoned the exchange enquiries to check my number in the cottage which most of Dehra Doon knows anyway. The operator told me quite abruptly that my telephone number did not exist and neither did I but I still receive bills. The chairman of ONGC kindly invited me for lunch, when I phoned to regret I was told that neither he nor his number existed. So India's biggest and most beneficial corporation has been wiped off the map.

It's Monday and Doon is on strike. When they can't find a public holiday, of which there are far too many, they invent a cause. In this case it was the incarceration of a seer, Shankacharya. According to newspaper reports, suspected of murder. 'How could anybody aged eighty commit murder?' asked Girl Monday. My mother-in-law aged ninety ceremoniously murders her servants everyday. But the newspaper article questioned whether the great British Public would tolerate the arrest of the Archbishop of Canterbury. They must be joking. They would laugh into their Sunday dinners. To correct an erroneous impression, few people in England know the name of the Archbishop of Canterbury and that he lives most of the time in the Palace of Lambeth on the south of the river Thames. Or that Queen Elizabeth, like the successive monarchs since Henry VII, have been titular heads of the Church of England. Henry in a fit of anger dissolved his relationship with the Roman Catholic Church as they objected to his repeated demands for divorces from his many wives. He found a perfect solution. He chopped off their heads then raided and looted the monasteries to pay for the wars against the French. Then, in true noble style, he converted the monasteries into schools, one of which I went to, the Kings school in Chester.

Great Excitement in the *khud* at the back of the cottage. Two mongooses had arrived. Unmistakable with their long snouty noses. Avaricious and indomitable executioners of snakes. So there are snakes in the *khud*. I call upon the villagers in the Rajpur Snake Village who arrived with aplomb with their musical mantras to add to their collection. They didn't find any. The mongooses have eaten them all. Today we had a new torment. Much to Freddy's and my neighbours dogs delight, a mass of mad monkey came chattering and swinging from one branch to the other. It was Happy Hour for Freddy. After an hour of frantic chase it was again Freddy's domain. The monkeys had left for the time being only leaving Freddy waiting for them anticipatorily. Basking in the November sun, yet another surprise. The goldfish under the waterfall have secretly blessed me with four grandchildren each one inch long. Little darling darting devils exploring their new home. Freddy is nonplussed. When will it be my turn? He growls.

39

But You Need Strong Bones to Survive a Gin or Three

Uttaranchal is never boring. Far from it. Like learning, to the delight of Girl Sunday and me, that Honey and Shamsher Singh's young grandson, has like his older brother, been admitted to Woodstock. Mother Cherry is over the moon. I trust the young lad will be allowed to take with him his turtles. But on condition that he moves faster through his classes.

Cricket. The great leveller especially between India and Pakistan. Of all the newspaper tales told, some apocryphal, some true and some apocalyptic, I had one from R.P. Eshwaran, a chartered accountant. It was a truly amazing account. A few late highlights even though the test series is not complete. At the Wagah border crossing, the Indian officials demanded facilitation money. One immigration desk for hundreds of fans. On the Pakistan side, rows of immigration desks each with bottled water and the procedure took two minutes, while the customs checked baggage for booze. Not that there is a shortage in Pakistan. Nor of, he said, the warmth of the welcome. No one could accept money for bottled water. The entrance to the Lahore stadium was in two queues. The Indian line was processed faster. And unlike European football, there was no crowd segregation. Indians and Pakistanis, newly acquired friends, swapped food, jokes and even knitted the Indian and Pakistani flags to jointly wave from the stands. Mr Eshwaran had been cautioned about Pakistanis: 'Don't bring your wife.' He wished that he had. And will certainly do so the next time. His and his companion's perception of the Pakistani people changed overnight. Was this spontaneous or contrived, I asked him seriously. Not even Tony Blair's spin doctor Alastair Campbell could have contrived this. Try waving the Pakistani flag at Eden gardens. You'll be crucified. So full marks to Prime Minister Vajpayee and to President Musharraf and to both teams for their successful attempt at cricket diplomacy. Although, I don't fancy Mr Vajpayee's chances at bowling against Musharraf. The former may need a runner.

Doon on a Sunday evening is curiously, but thankfully, quiet. The sun sinking reluctantly into the clear western sky. The waterfall muted while the fish cavort. Another six little tadpoles have arrived, four golden and two black. The herbaceous borders are now a riot of colours. Purple delphiniums, puce and pink vie for attention by the stream bed. The occasional poppy, ruby red. The first Flame of the Forest flower bursts over leafless trees and the bottle brush thickly clad in foliage, shyly emerge. The white oak is awaiting its turn. Meanwhile, the lychees are budding, *pomelos* in bloom. The *nimbus*, grapefruits and oranges flowering. This year I shall peel and can the mangoes. Freeze the jackfruit rissoles and devise a delight for the avocados.

It must be the calcium in our Doon water. I am no chemist, but understand from what the Americans would describe as reliable sources, that the Doon hills are made largely of limestone which contains calcium. A good friend, and true, Khalid Baig arrived from Delhi bearing cheese and other goodies. And stayed for a gin or three. He normally imbibes judiciously, but on leaving the cottage, managed inadvertently to slip on the river pebbles on the drive. Nursing his foot and resting awhile, having demurely denied another tot and self-diagnosing a twisted ankle, he left. Oh dear! Doctor Rajneesh Singh of Disha Hospital thought otherwise. The X-ray was conclusive. A broken foot. Ankles are worse, said Rajneesh morosely.

After my experience some years ago travelling in the South Atlantic on *HMS* Endurance, I developed an admiration for

Royal Navy officers, in particular those who enjoyed the sea. And, to join the Navy, why should not one. None in the officer's ward room ever thought they would achieve higher command than a destroyer. The carnival in Rio and penguins on the ice in South Georgia and the motto was from *HMS Pinafore* by Gilbert and Sullivan:

Stick close to your desks and never go to sea!
And you may end up rulers of the Queen's Navy.

April Toothpick award: this to Mr Tony Blair. A classic April Fool. For his confusing statements on outsourcing. Lloyds Bank in Pall Mall—previously in a historic building now occupied by the Bank of Nigeria and opposite a club frequented by directors of commerce—has moved many of its staff to Sunderland, not one of Britain's prettiest places. Damned difficult to get on the telephone unless one wishes to listen to endless recordings of *Greensleeves* which after the third rendering is not to my delight. And impossible to get to, on the train. And if you do, you will find everything closed because Sunderland City will be playing Newcastle United. So come all ye hopefuls to Secunderabad, Saharanpur and Sunnapalan. Enjoy Shining India. And if you don't like it, you can call Blair home.

40

To Sit on a Chair and Watch People Stare

On a Sunday afternoon, Dehra Doon muggy, Girl Sunday and I invited ourselves to tea at Sikander Hall, in Barlowgunj with Lillian and her sister Sylvia of the Skinner family. Sylvia's husband and Col Mahendroo and family. Tea was served in the traditional English manner. The pot nestling comfortably in it's cosy. Sandwiches and cheese straws. Mithai for the gluttons. And what folk stories! In Barlowgunj, when spiders climb up the wall, rains are expected. When they descend, expect an earthquake. When the sisters were young, their boyfriends could only afford to take them to Hackman's Hotel. Afterwards they would eat puri-bhaji at the corner stall, the bill amounting to two annas. What, we asked, about the Savoy Hotel. 'Snooty, said Lillian, 'We could never afford that'. But

Rupa

later, they would glide into the Savoy Hotel. The belles of the ball. Sad times now. Lillian had been to visit the Skinner family house in Haryana. 'Crumbling' she said, 'I could hear it'. So could the rats and they scampered faster.

Sunday evening arrives. Dusk falls. Safe from looming mountains, home to write. Sunday is tired. The bloody Deskjet won't print. Mother is waiting. Hers, not mine. Thank God for small mercies. I mutter sotto voce. Sunday, diminutive in size, but not in strength, looks at me speculatively, hammer in hand. The mother looks complacent.